SEXES AND GENEALOGIES

Luce Irigaray

SEXES AND GENEALOGIES

TRANSLATED BY GILLIAN C. GILL

Columbia University Press
NEW YORK

Columbia University Press wishes to express its appreci-
ation of assistance given by the government of France
through Le Ministère de la Culture in the preparation of
this translation.

Columbia University Press
New York   Chichester, West Sussex
Sexes et Parentés copyright © 1987 by Les Éditions de
Minuit
Copyright © 1993 Columbia University Press
All rights reserved

Library of Congress Cataloging-in-Publication Data

Irigaray, Luce.
[*Sexes et parentés*. English]
Sexes and genealogies / Luce Irigaray: translated by
Gillian C. Gill.
    p.   cm.
ISBN 0-231-07032-2
ISBN 0-231-07033-0 (pbk.)
1. Sex differences (Psychology)—History. 2. Women—
Psychology—History. 3. Feminist theology. I. Title.
BF692.2.I7413   1993   92-32495
155.3'3—dc20   CIP

Casebound editions of Columbia University Press books
are printed on permanent and durable acid-free paper.
Printed in the United States of America

c 10 9 8 7 6 5 4 3 2 1
p 10 9 8 7 6 5 4 3 2

Like my earlier book, Ethics of Sexual Difference,* *this volume is a collection of lectures. They were not all addressed to the same public, they were not all given in the same places and the same circumstances, and therefore there are variations in style, tone, and mode of development. The essential issue, however, is always whether it is possible to advance an ethics governing the relationship between the sexes. In this particular collection, the issue is discussed along the double axis of the genders as we know them today and as they have come into being over time—what I call their genealogies. No social and cultural relationship between the sexes is possible without that double consideration. Actually, our History has collapsed male and female genealogies into one or two family triangles, all sired by the male. The oedipus complex as elaborated by Freud is one example of such triangles. But Freud's model can be traced back at least as far as ancient Greece. In order to fuse two genealogical trees, it is always necessary to have recourse to a transcendent and unique God-Father. Sometimes his name is Zeus, sometimes Jupiter. He is also God the Father of Judeo-Christian tradition. Respect for God is possible as long as no one realizes that he is a mask concealing the fact that men have taken sole possession of the divine, of identity, and of kinship. Once we give this whole issue the attention and serious consideration it deserves, however, it becomes obvious that God is being used by men to oppress women and that, therefore, God must be questioned and not simply neutered in the current pseudoliberal way. Religion as a social phenomenon cannot be ignored. Marx fails to offer us any exhaustive guidance on this point, and his disciples risk perpetuating religious sectarianism and repression because they lack*

---

*Ithaca: Cornell University Press, translated by Carolyn Burke and Gillian C. Gill, forthcoming 1993.—Tr.

any adequate analysis of the materiality of culture and language. Claims that men, races, sexes, are equal in point of fact signal a disdain or a denial for real phenomena and give rise to an imperialism that is even more pernicious than those that retain traces of difference. Today it is all too clear that there is no equality of wealth, and claims of equal rights to culture have blown up in our faces. All those who advocate equality need to come to terms with the fact that their claims produce a greater and greater split between the so-called equal units and those authorities or transcendences used to measure or outmeasure them. Whether we like it or not, these authorities are still called capital or profit, and God(s), Man/Men. Any woman who is seeking equality (with whom? with what?) needs to give this problem serious consideration. It is understandable that women should wish for equal pay, equal career opportunities. But what is their real goal? It is all too easy to make the argument that women cannot do equal work because of pregnancy, child care, housework, etc. This does not mean that women should be paid less. It does mean that salaries and social recognition have to be negotiated on the basis of identity—not equality. Without women, there is no society. Women have to proclaim this message loud and clear and demand a justice that fits their identity instead of some temporary rights befitting justice for men. To achieve this goal, women must learn how they relate both to gender and to kinship. Sexual difference represents one of the great hopes for the future. It is not to be found in reproduction (whether natural or artificial) but in the access the two sexes have to culture. Childbearing is just one effect of this. If childbearing becomes a goal in itself, it often becomes confused with respect for nature. These lectures explain what misunderstandings and confusions are covered over by the reproductive mandate. Often reproduction takes the place of respect for nature and the world. In our day and age it seems less important to analyze where the split between nature and culture occurs than to mark the places where growth has been sterilized, misunderstood, repressed. Our culture has in some ways become too simple, in other ways too complex. We need to regain places where measure is possible, and I believe this can be done if we look at the cultural becoming of the sexes, as defined in relation to their genealogies.

The first four of these lectures have already been published. For this collection I have reread and revised them as they bring special light to bear on the lectures that follow, particularly in regard to the psycho-socio-religious dimension. My goal in this volume is also to conjure up the communities, the cities, the places where these lectures were given and thus to make them better known. The essays in this collection for the most part present the material as it was offered to the public on first occasions. My thanks go out to all the people who invited me to speak and engage in cultural exchange with them.

CONTENTS-CALENDAR OF LECTURES

EACH SEX
MUST HAVE ITS OWN RIGHTS

In the field of law, one sector that is currently mutating is the relationship between the male and female sexes, particularly insofar as the family and its relation to reproduction are concerned. Our cultures are seeing changes in the laws relating to the obligation to bear children, the right to contraception and abortion, the choice of name for women and children within the marriage, freedom to choose a domicile for the members of the couple, the relevance of paying a salary for housework, length of maternity leaves, protection for women in the workplace, etc. These measures cut across lines of natural law, penal codes, civil codes, religious law. Little thought is given to what the whole field represented by these different parts might mean.

Hegel did take on the project of interpreting how a whole society or culture might function. His aim was to describe and work out how the *Geist* or spirit of man as individual and as citizen functioned. The weakest link in his system seems to lie in his interpretation of spirit and right within the family. Even though he consistently sought to break up undifferentiated units, Hegel is unable to think of the family as anything but a single substance within which particular individuals lose their rights. Except the right to life, perhaps? Which is not that simple. . . .

THE ORIGIN OF THE FAMILY . . .

In the chapter of *The Phenomenology of Mind* that deals with the family, Hegel concentrates the first part of his analysis on the relation of man to spirit in culture. The chapter initially concerns the issue of ethics and their relation to morality. In this passage Hegel says something very important about the right of genders. Yet this seems to have been lost in the implications Hegel draws about the spirit of the people (*Volk*) and of peoples.

What is the issue here? In the analyses he devotes to the family as it relates to the state, Hegel explains that the daughter who remains

1

faithful to the laws relating to her mother has to be cast out of the city, out of society. She cannot be violently killed, but she must be imprisoned, deprived of liberty, air, light, love, marriage, children. In other words, she is condemned to a slow and lonely death. The character Antigone represents that daughter. Hegel's analysis is supported by the content of Sophocles's tragedies.

What is the nature of the laws that Antigone respects? They are religious laws relating to the burial of her brother who has been killed in a war among men. These laws have to do with the cultural obligations owed to the mother's blood, the blood shared by the brothers and sisters in the family. The duty to this blood will be denied and outlawed as the culture becomes patriarchal. This tragic episode in life—and in war—between the genders represents the passage into patriarchy. The daughter is forbidden to respect the blood bonds with her mother. From the spiritual viewpoint, these bonds have a religious quality, they move in consonance with the fertility of the earth and its flowers and fruits, they protect love in its bodily dimension, they keep watch over female fruitfulness within and without marriage (depending on whether the kingdom of Aphrodite or of Demeter is invoked), they correspond to times of peace.

Under the rule of patriarchy the girl is separated from her mother and from her family in general. She is transplanted into the genealogy of her husband; she must live with him, carry his name, bear his children, etc. The first time that this takes place, the move is recorded as the abduction of a woman by a man-lover. A war breaks out among men to recapture the stolen woman and bring her back to her community of origin.

Our code of morality today is still derived from those very ancient events. This means that the love between mother and daughter, which the patriarchal regime has made impossible (as Freud in fact reinforces for our benefit), has been transformed into the woman's obligation to devote herself to the cult of the children of her legal husband and to the husband himself as a male child. In fact, despite the incest taboo, there seems little indication that man has sublimated the natural immediacy of his relationship to the mother. Rather, man has transferred that relationship to his wife as mother substitute. In this way the man-woman couple is always out of phase by a generation, since male and female genealogies are collapsed into a single genealogy: that of the *husband.*

2

THE DOUBLE MEANING OF THE WORD NATURE

The achievements recorded by recent movements for women's liberation have failed to establish a new *ethics* of sexuality. They nonetheless serve notice to us that ethics is the crucial issue because they have released so much violent, undirected energy, desperate for an outlet. They fall back into unmediated naturalness: the obligation to give birth, violence barely channeled into sado-masochistic scenarios, regression to animality (with no display?) in the erotic act, fear and destructiveness between the sexes. . . .

Obviously, I am not advocating a return to a more repressive, moralizing, conception of sexuality. On the contrary, what we need is to work out an art of the sexual, a sexed culture, instead of merely using our bodies to release neuropsychic tensions and produce babies.

When women are forced to bear children within the genealogy of the husband, this historically marks the beginning of a *failure of respect for nature*. A new notion or concept of nature is set up, which takes the place of earth's fertility, abandons its religious quality, its link to the divinity of women and to the mother-daughter relation. Paradoxically, the cult of the mother in our cultures today is often associated with a scorn or neglect of nature. It is true that in patriarchal genealogy we are dealing with the cult of the *son's mother*, to the detriment of the daughter's mother. The cult of the son's mother ties our tradition into the whole mother-son incest issue and the taboo upon it. Our societies forget fascination with that incest leads us to neglect the genealogy of the woman, which has been collapsed inside the man's.

Once one genealogy has been reduced to the other's, it becomes impossible or at least difficult for the casual thinker to define two different genders or sexes. Man takes his orientation from his relation to his father insofar as his name and property are concerned and from his mother in relation to unmediated nature. Woman must submit to her husband and to reproduction. This means that gender as sexuality is never sublimated. *Gender is confused with species.* Gender becomes the human race, human nature, etc., as defined from within patriarchal culture. Gender thus defined corresponds to a race of men (*un peuple d'hommes*) who refuse, whether consciously or not, the possibility of another gender: the female. All that is left is the human race/gender (*le genre humain*) for which the only real value of sex is to reproduce the species. From this point of view, *gender is always subservient to kinship.* Man and woman would not come to maturity with a thinking and a culture relative to the sexual difference of each. They would be more or less sexed children and adolescents, and then reproductive adults. In this perspective, the family serves the interests of property, of material patrimony, and of the reproduction of children. The family is not a small unit in which individual differences can be respected and cultivated.

As for life, the conclusion is inevitable that rights are unequally distributed and frequently turn into duties, especially for women: the duty to bear children, sexual duties. No legislation offers women protection. This anomaly is often accounted for by the power of religious morality in questions of social practice and reproduction. This influence, which is the residue of ancient gynocratic traditions, is marked today by patriarchal imperatives: give property to the husband, children to the State. . . .

We need to reinterpret the idea of nature that underlies such imperatives. Often, it is less a question of life than of an idea of life and of a valid lifestyle. But value, and values, have been codified in the men's camp: they are not appropriate to women, or not appropriated by them. The law has not been written to defend the life and property of women. A few partial changes in rights for women have been won in recent times. But even these are subject to recall. They are won by partial and local pressures whereas what is needed is a full-scale rethinking of the law's duty to offer justice to *two genders that differ* in their needs, their desires, their properties.

SEX AS AN ETHICAL DIMENSION

When faced by questions such as these, many men and women start talking about *love.* But love is only possible when there are two parties and in a relationship that is not submissive to one gender, not subject to reproduction. It requires that the rights of both male and female be written into the legal code. If the rights of the couple were indeed written into the legal code, this would serve to convert individual morality into collective ethics, to transform the relations of the genders within the family or its substitute into rights and duties that involve the culture as a whole. Religion can then rediscover how each gender interprets its relation to the divine—a religion freed from its role of guardian of a single gender and financial trustee for the property of one gender more than of the other. Hardly a godly role! Furthermore, once the rights of each gender have been written into the legal documents representing society or culture, this will mean that natural law is no longer separate from civil law, and that a concrete private law is set up that takes the daily needs of each one of us into account. What does the right to private property mean when excessive noise and odor pollution and the organized violence of the media, etc., destroy the sense *perceptions* indispensable for life and mind? Such a law is merely an abstract demand, based on money and careless of the bodies, love, and intelligence of the men and women who share an often limited and expensive living space.

Such living conditions do not contribute to the development of human peoples. How often our nerves are set on edge. We are driven to compete in the rat race of modern life—so maddened and overwhelmed by the pace of existence that we embrace war as a means of regaining some measure of order and opening some new space onto the future. This was often true in the past. It will continue to be so if we fail to set up an ethics of the couple as an intermediary place between individuals, peoples, States. Wars break out when peoples move too far from their natural possibilities, when abstract energy builds up so much that it can no longer be controlled by subjects or reduced to one or more concrete responsibilities. Collective madness, then, is the name we give to the concrete, sacrificial goal we set in order to reduce the rising tide of abstraction.

In the exercise of a social and cultural ethics that acknowledged sexual difference, History might find a more continuous course of development, one less subject to periodic expansions and reductions that defy society's control.

BODY AGAINST BODY:
IN RELATION TO THE MOTHER

Montreal, May 31, 1980
Fifth Conference on Mental Health
in the province of Quebec,
entitled "Women and Madness"

I should like to begin by thanking the organizing committee of the conference on mental health for choosing "Women and Madness" as the theme of this meeting and for thus playing some part in breaking the silence and invisibility that afflict so many women.

I am surprised—and, sadly, am not at all surprised! but I prefer to keep on being surprised—that so few male practitioners have come to the conference today to hear what women have to say about their madness. Most women are treated by male physicians, and the absence of these men already tells us something about their practice, particularly their psychiatric practice. They seem to have so little interest in what women say. To establish a diagnosis and prescribe a treatment, men need only each other. Why bother listening to the female patient? This attitude goes far to explain the therapeutic choices available to these male doctors.

Yet how often have I heard men say how annoying it is that women get together for meetings and how much they, the men, would like to be able to attend and find out what is going on. So their absence here today is all the more significant. They were not excluded from this conference, at which women speakers would be in the majority. Why hasn't their curiosity brought them here? The few men who are in attendance today should make an effort to try and understand how and why they come to be exceptions!

Could it be that those other men, the majority of practitioners, have refrained from coming because of the power issue? Men are not leading this conference. Or are they simply ashamed to make an appearance, in light of the statistics offered this morning on the frightening number of women committed to psychiatric institutions (usually committed by their families, with the hospital serving as a

The title of this speech or essay, "Le corps-à-corps avec la mère," has no simple translation in English. The expression *corps-à-corps*, which recurs throughout the text, usually denotes armed combat between two warriors—hand-to-hand fighting. However, it is the word *corps* (body) that is crucial to Irigaray, who is looking to some new relationship between mother and child that accepts the body of both parties and moves toward a new imaginary and a new symbolic.—Tr.

place of incarceration) who are then treated with chemotherapy, not psychotherapy? Unless it is all a matter of professional disdain for a conference organized by and for women? Or of sexual indifference? I leave the interpretation open.

In any case, the absence of male doctors is, in and of itself, one explanation of madness in women: their words are not heard. Women and their words are not given the keys to the city when it comes to developing the diagnoses and therapeutic decisions that concern them. Serious scientific discourse and practice remain the privilege of men who have control of politics in general as well as of our most private sphere as women. Everywhere, in everything, men's speech, men's values, dreams, and desires are law. Everywhere and in everything men define the function and the social role of women, right down to the sexual identity that women are to have—or not to have. Men know, men have access to the truth, not us. We barely, at times, have access to fiction!

Rather to his own surprise, one particularly "honest" male friend admitted to me not long ago: "You know, you're right. I always thought that all women were mad." And he added: "Obviously that was one way of avoiding the issue of my own madness."

This is in fact how the question needs to be posed. Each sex has a relation to madness. Every desire has a relation to madness. But it would seem that one desire has been taken as wisdom, moderation, truth, leaving to the other sex the weight of a madness that cannot be acknowledged or accommodated.

This relation of desire to madness works in a privileged manner in the relation to the mother, for man as well as for woman. But all too often man rids himself of that madness and unloads it upon woman—or women.

The relation to the mother is a mad desire, because it is the "dark continent" par excellence. It remains in the shadow of our culture, it is night and hell. But men cannot do without it anymore than—or perhaps less than—women can. And if today's society is so polarized by the issues of contraception and abortion, surely this reflects the need to escape the question of the imaginary and symbolic relation to the mother, to the woman-mother. What is woman, apart from her social and material function in reproducing children, nursing, renewing the work force?

The maternal function underlies the social order as well as the order of desire) but it is always restricted to the dimension of need. Once individual and collective needs have been met there is often nothing left of maternal female potency to satisfy desire, particularly in its religious dimension.

Her desire, the desire she has, this is what the law of the father, of all fathers, moves to prohibit: the fathers of families, fathers in religion, father teachers, father doctors, father lovers, etc. Whether moral or immoral, all these fathers intervene to censure, repress, the mother's desire. For them, it's a matter of good sense, good health, or even of virtue and holiness!

Perhaps we have reached a period in history when this question of the father's dominance can no longer be avoided. The prominence of this question is the result, at least in part, of several factors. Contraception and abortion raise the issue of the meaning of motherhood, and women (notably because they have gained access to the market) are in search of their sexual identity and are beginning to emerge from silence and anonymity.

One thing is plain, not only in everyday events but in the whole social scene: our society and our culture operate on the basis of an original matricide.

When Freud, notably in *Totem and Taboo*, describes and theorizes about the murder of the father as the founding act for the primal horde, he is forgetting an even more ancient murder, that of the woman-mother, which was necessary to the foundation of a specific order in the city.

With a few additions and subtractions, our imaginary still works according to the schema set in place by Greek mythology and tragedy. I shall therefore take the example of Clytemnestra's murder in the *Oresteia*.

Quite obviously, Clytemnestra does not conform to that image of the virgin-mother which has been promoted as our ideal for centuries. She is still passionately a lover. She will in fact go so far as to kill for love: she will kill her husband. But why?

For years and years her husband has been away from home, off with other men to recapture the fair Helen. This is perhaps the prototype of war among men. In order to secure his military and amorous expedition, Agamemnon sacrificed Iphigenia, the adolescent daughter he had with Clytemnestra. When he returns home, it is with another girl by his side, Cassandra, his slave and, no doubt, the latest in his string of mistresses.

Clytemnestra, for her part, has taken a lover. But she believed her husband was dead, since she had been without news of him for many years. When Agamemnon returns in triumph with his mistress she kills him. She kills him out of jealousy, out of fear perhaps, and because she has been dissatisfied and frustrated for so long. She also kills him because he has sacrificed their daughter in the cause of male conflicts, though this motive is often forgotten by the authors of tragedy.

But the new order decrees that she be killed in her turn by her son, who is inspired to do so by the oracle of Apollo, beloved son of Zeus: the God-Father. Orestes kills his mother because the empire of the God-Father, who has seized and taken for his own the ancient powers (*puissances*)* of the earth-mother, demands it. He kills his mother and is driven mad, as is his sister Electra.

Electra, the daughter, will remain mad. The matricidal son, on the other hand, must be saved from madness so that he can found the patriarchal order. The fair Apollo, lover of men rather than women, narcissistic lover of their bodies and their words, a lover who in fact does not make love much more often than his sister in Zeus, Athena, helps Orestes shake off his madness.

Madness is in fact represented in the shape of a horde of angry women, the Erinnyes, who pursue Orestes, haunting him at every step, almost like ghosts of his mother. These women howl for revenge. Together they hunt down the son who has killed his mother. They are women in rebellion, types of hysterical revolutionaries who rise up against the patriarchal power that is being established.

As you will have noticed, this whole story is extremely topical. The mythology that underlies patriarchy has not changed. Everything described in the *Oresteia* is still taking place. Here and there we still see the emergence of some useful Athenas, who spring whole from the brain of the Father-King, dedicated solely to his service and that of the men in power. They bury the women who fight patriarchy under the sanctuary so as to eliminate any troublesome challenge to the new order laid down for households, the order of the city-state, the only order from now on. These useful Athenas, perfect models of femininity, always veiled and clothed from head

---

* Modern French has two more or less interchangeable words for *power: le pouvoir* and *la puissance*. Irigaray makes a practice of distinguishing the two. *Le pouvoir* in her work is used for power in general and associated with patriarchy. *La puissance* is associated with women, is used for ancient female authority and tradition as well as for the possible new, feminized, world order, and has positive connotations. As English has no equivalent pairing, the French will appear parenthetically when Irigaray uses *puissance*.—Tr.

to toe, very respectable, can be recognized by this sign: they are extraordinarily attractive—which doesn't mean they attract—but they really aren't interested in making love.

Thus the murder of the mother is rewarded by letting the son go scot free, by burying the madness of women—and burying women in madness—and by introducing the image of the virgin goddess, born of the Father, obedient to his laws at the expense of the mother.

In fact, when Oedipus makes love to his mother one might say that he does so at first with impunity. On the other hand, he will become blind or mad as soon as he knows that it was his mother: whom he has already killed, according to his mythology, in obedience to the verdict of the Father of the gods.

This is a possible interpretation, although it is never offered. Inevitably the story is accounted for in terms of taking the place of the father and the symbolic murder of the father. Yet, Oedipus clearly reactualizes the madness of Orestes. He is afraid of his mother when she reveals herself to him as his mother. His original crime is echoed back to him, he fears and loathes his act, and the woman who was the target of that act. Only on a secondary level does he infringe upon the law of the father.

Every theory and practice derived from psychoanalysis seems to be based upon the ambivalence that Oedipus feels toward his father. An ambivalence that aims at the father but is projected retroactively upon the primitive relation to the mother's body. Now, it is true that, in so far as it takes account of the drives, analysis does have things to tell us about the mother's breast, about the milk she offers, about the feces she takes away (a "gift" she is more or less interested in), and even about her gaze and her voice. But analysis shows too little interest in these things. Furthermore, isn't it true that all this wrestling (*corps-à-corps*) with the mother, which has difficulties of its own, is part of a postoedipal phantasy projected backward onto the Oedipus phase? When the mother is cut up in stages, when each part of her body has to be cathected and then decathected if the child is to grow, she has already been torn to pieces by the hatred of Oedipus. And when Freud talks about the father being torn apart by the sons in the primeval horde, isn't he, out of full-scale denial and misunderstanding, forgetting the woman who has been torn between son and father, among sons?

The *partial* drives, in fact, seem to refer especially to the body that brought us *whole* into the world. The genital drive is theoretically that drive by which the phallic penis captures the mother's power to give birth, nourish, inhabit, center. Doesn't the phallic erection occur at the place where the umbilical cord once was? The phallus becomes the organizer of the world through the man-father at the very place where the umbilical cord, that primal link to the mother, once gave birth to man and woman. All that had taken place within an originary womb, the first nourishing earth, first waters, first sheaths, first membranes in which the *whole* child was held, as well as the *whole* mother, through the mediation of her blood. According to a relationship that is obviously not symmetrical, mother and child are linked in a way that precedes all dissociations, all tearing of their bodies into pieces.

This primary experience is very unpopular with psychoanalysts: in fact they refuse to see it. They allude to a fetal situation or fetal regression and find nothing to say about it. A vague sort of taboo is in force. There would be a danger of fusion, death, lethal sleep, if the father did not intervene to sever this uncomfortably close link to the original matrix. Does the father replace the womb with the matrix of his language? But the exclusivity of his law refuses all representation to that first body, that first home, that first love. These are sacrificed and provide matter for an empire of language that so privileges the male sex as to confuse it with the human race.

The order of this empire decrees that when a proper name (*nom*) is given to a child, it substitutes for the most irreducible mark of birth, the navel (*nombril*). The family name, and even the first or given name, always stand at one remove from that most elemental identity tag: the scar where the umbilical cord was cut. The family name, and even the first name, slip over the body like clothes, like identity tags—outside the body.

Nonetheless, in psychoanalysis however much use is made of the law, of the symbolic, of language, and of the family name (the father's name), the analyst in therapy generally sits behind the analysand, like the mother toward whom the analysand is forbidden to turn. The patient must move forward, ahead, out, by forgetting the mother. And if he did turn around, perhaps she might have disappeared? Perhaps he has annihilated her?

The social order, our culture, psychoanalysis itself, are all insistent that the mother must remain silent, outlawed. The father forbids any *corps-à-corps* with the mother.

14

I am tempted to add: if only this were really true! We would be more at peace with our bodies if it were, and men need peace to feed their libido as well as their life and culture. For the ban does not prevent a certain number of failures of compliance, a certain blindness.

And where are we to find the imaginary and symbolic of life in the womb and the first *corps-à-corps* with the mother? In what darkness, what madness, do they lie abandoned?

And the relation to the placenta, that first home that surrounds us and whose aura accompanies our every step, like a primary safety zone, how is that presented to us in our culture? No image has been formed for the placenta and hence we are constantly in danger of retreating into the original matrix, of seeking refuge in any open body, and forever nestling into the body of other women.

In this way the opening of the mother, the opening to the mother, appear as threats of contagion, contamination, falling into sickness, madness, death. Obviously, there is nothing available that can allow us to move forward firmly without risk. No Jacob's ladder is there to help us climb back to the mother. Jacob's ladder always moves up to heaven, toward the father and his kingdom.

And who in fact would credit the innocence of this bond with the mother, since anyone who seeks to reestablish that bond with her will be accused of the crime that has repeatedly been committed against her?

The devouring monster we have turned the mother into is an inverted reflection of the blind consumption that she is forced to submit to. Her womb, sometimes her breast, gape open as a result of the gestation, the birthing, the life which have issued from them, without reciprocity. Unless murder, whether real or cultural, serves to erase the debt? forget the dependency? destroy the power (*puissance*)?

The insatiable character of what we in psychotherapy call orality, the unquenchable thirst, the desire for the mother to fill us to the brim, is the subject of much discussion in analysis, and may make certain cures impossible. Yet is this characterization of the infant's mouth—or the woman's sex—as a bottomless pit not a thought or a phantasy derived from oedipal hatred? There is no real reason to believe that an infant's thirst or a woman's sexuality is insatiable. All the evidence is to the contrary. But that mouth cavity of the child, like any desire, becomes a bottomless pit if the time spent in

15

Use oral hatred article →

utero is a taboo issue and if no attempt is made to interpret and come to terms with the losses and the scars involved in our separation from that primary home and that first nurse. The child demands that the breast offer him everything. The everything that he once received in his mother's womb: life, home, both the home of his own body and of the mother's body that he inhabits, food, air, warmth, movement, etc. This everything is displaced into oral avidity because there is no way to place it in its space, its time, and the exile from both. The wound we can never heal, never cure, opens up when the umbilical cord is severed. When the father or the mother threaten Oedipus with scissors or knife, they forget that the cord, already, has been cut and that all that is needed is to take cognizance of that fact.

The problem is that when the father refuses to allow the mother her power of giving birth and seeks to be the sole creator, then according to our culture he superimposes upon our ancient world of flesh and blood a universe of language and symbols that has no roots in the flesh and drills a hole through the female womb and through the place of female identity. A stake, an axis is thus driven into the earth in order to mark out the boundaries of the sacred space in many patriarchal traditions. It defines a meeting place for men that is based upon an immolation. Women will in the end be allowed to enter that space, provided that they do so as nonparticipants.

The fertility of the earth is sacrificed in order to establish the cultural domain of the father's language (which is called, incorrectly, the mother tongue). But this is never spoken of. Just as the scar of the navel is forgotten, so, correspondingly, a hole appears in the texture of the language.

Some men and women would prefer to identify maternal power, the phallic mother, as an ensnaring net. But such attribution occurs only as a defensive mesh that the man-father or his sons casts over the chasms of a silent and threatening womb. Threatening because it is silent, perhaps?

The womb is never thought of as the primal place in which we become body. Therefore for many men it is variously phantasized as a devouring mouth, as a sewer in which anal and urethral waste is poured, as a threat to the phallus or, at best, as a reproductive organ. And the womb is mistaken for all the female sexual organs since no valid representations of female sexuality exist.

The only words we have for women's sexuality are filthy, mutilating words. Consequently, the feelings associated with women's sex-

16

uality will be anxiety, phobia, disgust, and the haunting fear of castration.

How are any other feelings possible when we are asked to move back toward something that has always been negated, denied, sacrificed for the construction of an exclusively male symbolic world?

Is it possible that castration anxiety is an unconscious reminder of the sacrifice that consecrated the phallic erection as unique sexual value? But neither the postulation nor the name of the father suffices to guarantee that the son's penis will remain erect. And it is not the murder of the father that both sustains and threatens the phallic erection, despite the claims made by patriarchal tradition in a kind of act of faith.

Unless—but this never crosses the threshold of thought—this murder of the father means not a desire to take the father's place as rival and competitor, but a desire instead to do away with the one who has artificially severed the bond with the mother in order to take over the power of creating any world, particularly a female one.

According to this interpretation, phallic erection, far from being all-powerful, would be the masculine version of the umbilical cord. If phallic erection respected the life of the mother—of the mother in every women and of the woman in every mother—it would repeat the living bond to the mother. At the very place where there once had been the cord, then the breast, would in due time appear, for the man, the penis which reconnects, gives life, feeds and recenters the bodies. The penis evokes something of the life within the womb as it stiffens, touches, and spills out, passing beyond the skin and the will. As it softens and falls, it evokes the end, mourning, the ever open wound. Men would be performing an act of anticipatory repetition, a return to the world that allows them to become sexual adults capable of eroticism and reciprocity in the flesh.

This return to the world is also necessary for women. It can take place only if woman is released from the archaic projections man lays upon her and if an autonomous and positive representation of female sexuality exists in the culture.

Woman has no cause to envy the penis or the phallus. But because of the failure to establish a sexual identity for both sexes— man, and the race of men, has transformed the male organ into an instrument of power with which to master maternal power (*puissance*).

☆

17

What is useful to women in all these descriptions? When we are able to understand and interpret all of this, we are empowered to leave a world of madness that is not our own, cease to fear the night, the unidentifiable, a fear of an originary murder that is culturally not ours. I think it is very important to take cognizance of all this, because we are still defined by these projections even today. Even today we become the slaves of those phantasies, of that ambivalence, that madness, which is not ours. Let us rather take new hold of our own madness and leave men theirs!

Our urgent task is to refuse to submit to a desubjectivized social role, the role of mother, which is dictated by an order subject to the division of labor—he produces, she reproduces—that walls us up in the ghetto of a single function. When did society ever ask fathers to choose between being men or citizens? We don't have to give up being women to be mothers.

One other point, since my purpose is to set out a number of issues to open up discussion. We also need to discover and declare that we are always mothers just by being women. We bring many things into the world apart from children, we give birth to many other things apart from children: love, desire, language, art, social things, political things, religious things, but this kind of creativity has been forbidden to us for centuries. We must take back this maternal creative dimension that is our birthright as women.

If birthing is not to become traumatizing and pathological, the question of having or not having children should always be raised in the context of another birthing, a creation of images and symbols. Both women and their children would benefit enormously from this.

We need to be careful in one other respect: not again to kill the mother who was immolated at the birth of our culture. Our task is to give life back to that mother, to the mother who lives within us and among us. We must refuse to allow her desire to be swallowed up in the law of the father. We must give her the right to pleasure, to sexual experience, to passion, give her back the right to speak, or even to shriek and rage aloud.

We also need to find, rediscover, invent the words, the sentences that speak of the most ancient and most current relationship we know—the relationship to the mother's body, to our body—sentences

18

that translate the bond between our body, her body, the body of our daughter. We need to discover a language that is not a substitute for the experience of *corps-à-corps* as the paternal language seeks to be, but which accompanies that bodily experience, clothing it in words that do not erase the body but speak the body.

It is crucial that we keep our bodies even as we bring them out of silence and servitude. Historically we are the guardians of the flesh. We should not give up that role, but identify it as our own, by inviting men not to make us into body for their benefit, not to make us into guarantees that their body exists. All too often the male libido needs some woman (wife-mother) to guard the male body. This is why men need a wife in the home, even when they have a mistress elsewhere. This is a very important issue, even if it seems harmless.

Thus it is desirable that we should speak as we are making love. We should also speak as we feed a baby so that the child does not feel that the milk is being stuffed down his or her throat, in a kind of rape. It is equally important for us to speak as we caress another body. Silence is all the more alive when words exist. Let us not become the guardians of dumb silence, of dead silence.

If we are not to be accomplices in the murder of the mother we also need to assert that there is a genealogy of women. Each of us has a female family tree: we have a mother, a maternal grandmother and great-grandmothers, we have daughters. Because we have been exiled into the house of our husbands, it is easy to forget the special quality of the female genealogy; we might even come to deny it. Let us try to situate ourselves within that female genealogy so that we can win and hold on to our identity. Let us not forget, moreover, that we already have a history, that certain women, despite all the cultural obstacles, have made their mark upon history and all too often have been forgotten by us.

What this amounts to is that we need above all (though there's no one thing that has to be done before another) to discover our sexual identity, the specialness of our desires, of our autoeroticism, our narcissism, our heterosexuality, our homosexuality. In this context it is important to remind ourselves that, since the first body we as women had to relate to was a woman's body and our first love is love of the mother, women always have an ancient and primary relationship to what is called homosexuality. Men, on the other hand, always have an ancient relationship to heterosexuality, since their first love object is a woman.

When analytic theory claims that the little girl must give up her love for and of the mother, abandon the desire for and of her mother, if she is to enter into desire for the father, woman is thereby subjected to a normative heterosexuality, common in our societies, but nonetheless completely pathogenic and pathological. Neither the little girl nor the woman needs to give up the love for her mother. To do so is to sever women from the roots of their identity and their subjectivity.

Let us also try to discover the special character of our love for other women. This could be called (though I hate labels), between lots of quotation marks: " " "secondary homosexuality." " " I am trying in this way to make a distinction between the ancient love for the mother and the love for sister-women. This love is essential if we are to quit our common situation and cease being the slaves of the phallic cult, commodities to be used and exchanged by men, competing objects in the marketplace.

We need to discover what makes our experience of sexual pleasure special. Obviously, it is possible for a woman to use the phallic model of sexual pleasure and there's no lack of men or pornographers to tell women that they can achieve extraordinary sexual pleasure within that phallic economy. The question remains: doesn't that economy draw women out of themselves and leave them without energy, perceptions, affects, gestures, and images that refer to their own identity? There are at least two modes of sexual pleasure for women. The first is programmed into a male libidinal economy and obeys a certain phallic order. Another is much more in harmony with what women are, with their sexual identity. Many women feel guilty, unhappy, frozen, and claim to be frigid because they are unable to live their affects, their sexuality, in the framework of a phallocratic economy. These same women would no longer be frigid if they tried to reconnect with a sexual pleasure more suited to their bodies and their sexual resources. This does not mean that women should always and instantly give up the other. I have no wish to force any woman to make choices that risk becoming repressive in their turn. But I think it is important, if we are to discover our female identity, for us to know that another relation to sexual pleasure is available apart from the phallic model.

We have a great deal to do. But how much better to have a future in front of us, rather than some new version of the past. Let us not wait for the god Phallus to give us his grace. The god Phallus, indeed, because even though many people go around saying God is dead, few would question the fact that the Phallus is alive and well. And don't many of the bearers of the said phallus walk around today claiming to be gods no less? They are everywhere, even—and here I shall raise my final question—in the holy Roman Catholic church where the Holy Father the Pope believes it right to forbid us once again: contraception, abortion, extramarital relations, homosexuality, etc. And yet, when the minister of that one and only God, that God-Father, pronounces the words of the Eucharist: "This is my body, this is my blood," according to the rite that celebrates the sharing of food and that has been ours for centuries, perhaps we might remind him that he would not be there if our body and our blood had not given him life, love, spirit. And that he is also serving us up, we women-mothers, on his communion plate. But this is something that must not be known. That is why women cannot celebrate the Eucharist. . . . If they were to do so, something of the truth that is hidden in the communion rite would be brutally unmasked.

At the same moment the human race would be absolved of a great offense. If a woman were to celebrate the Eucharist with her mother, giving her a share of the fruits of the earth blessed by them both, she might be freed from all hatred or ingratitude toward her maternal genealogy, and be hallowed in her identity as a woman.

BELIEF ITSELF

Cerisy-la-Salle, August 10, 1980
Conference on the work of Jacques Derrida:
The Ends of Man

What I am about to tell you, or confide in you, today, will remain rather primary, loose. This is both deliberate and due to lack of time. But what time do I mean? The time that has not, or has not yet, been loosed by all that is too bound, too secondarily bound, thereby leaving so-called free energy chained up, in the crypt. But perhaps that energy is merely deprived of the space-time it needs to cathect, unfold, inscribe, play. . . .

So I shall be talking more or less freely, offering to your associations and interpretations certain of the still dark, oneiric experiences, trials, associations that I have had as woman and as analyst. At times it will be like a children's story.

To dream greatly, to hold onto sleep while letting everything float freely, is, among other things, the duty or the vocation of the analyst. Especially if she is a woman, perhaps. Bound and chained in and under the secondary processes? A "poste restante" or P.O. box[1] where messages for unknown persons with no fixed address are held, undeliverable by the usual, already coded, telecommanded, circuits.

So, at this poste restante, a woman's message came my way recently that could not be decoded by the usual interpretative methods. The woman told me she had given the message to one psychoanalyst with no success—no useful interpretation was afforded, they both agreed. The resistance set up by the analyst, by analysis, by the woman herself perhaps, was too strong, the associations were confused and confusing, a deaf ear was turned to such events.

Yet, this message is in my opinion the essential preliminary for any consideration of sexual difference. It tells us where the obstacle lies. What it is that lies across the threshold, blocking access, barring the very location.

Here is the message: "At the point in the mass when they, the

1. This allusion to the postal service will become clear later.

(spiritual) father and son, are reciting together the ritual words of the consecration, saying, 'This is my body, this is my blood,' I bleed."[2]

The father and the son must celebrate the Eucharist together in her absence, and then hand out the consecrated bread and wine to the congregation to complete the communion service. This generally occurs on a Sunday. She makes the connection between her hemorrhaging and the mass only subsequently.

She adds that she loves the son. At least consciously, secondarily, she does not accept the men's current forms of belief. This is not to say that she is alien to that aspect of the divine which finds an impoverished form and fulfillment in their celebrations—a divine that comes as blood flowing *over and above*. The truth of father and son assails her, wounds her in that place where she remains excluded from the manifestation of their faith, though she is not necessarily far outside their tradition. Her fidelity to that tradition is shown in a sensual experience for which the words, the rites, the historic interpretation of the texts, are inadequate. It finds expression in a bodily immediacy that no mediation the woman knows can affect.

In her turn, she fears not being believed, even by herself, and goes so far as to look for proofs and demonstrations! Nothing changes. No word comes, or at least none that matches her problem, her sense of abandonment.

First association for me: what deceives some people and destroys others about belief is the way it makes us forget the real. Faith first stands in for confidence and loyalty, and then it aims to double its own reflection, to square or even cube all its numbers or letters and thereby make the other—with a capital *O*—the other of the same. But, for this to succeed, surely a sacrifice of a different body and flesh is made? Yet no one must ever see that, by means of the male twosome, it is she who is being offered in partial oblation, she who manages the communion between them and among the other men and women present.[3]

---

2. It seems difficult, I think, to establish that these two events happen at exactly the same time. On the other hand, there is no question that the onset of bleeding coincides with the hour of the eucharistic celebration and the approximate moment when the host is consecrated.

3. The situation might be susceptible to sex permutations, but asymmetrically. That which is offered to be partaken is always a maternal body, unless we were to say equally: this is my sperm. It is worth considering why that formula is never used. Could it be that the eucharistic rite is bound up with an imaginary of the prenatal stage and earliest infancy?

Belief is safe only if that in which or in whom the assembly communes or communicates is subject to concealment. Once this is exposed, there is no need to believe, at least as adherence is usually understood. But truth, any truth throughout the centuries, assumes a belief that undermines it and that seduces and numbs anyone who believes. Does not the fact that this belief asserts and unveils itself in the form of religious myths, dogmas, figures, or rites show us that metaphysics keeps watch over the crypt of faith? Theology and the ritual practices it demands would seem to correspond to one formulation of all that is hidden in the constitution of the monocratic patriarchal truth, the faith in its order, its word, its logic.

Therefore I shall term the preliminary to the question of sexual difference: belief itself.

Let me go back to my example. This woman I spoke of, whose age casts her as mother and daughter, between mother and daughter, tells me: I bleed. This is truly a strange *I*. It takes place both outside and inside the game, but in a radical hemmorhage of herself. She is faraway when she bleeds. She needs to be faraway when that (*ça*) takes place, too far to come back to him, to her, within herself, kept at a distance from the celebration and the communion that occurs between the men, among the men and the women.

These are the facts. With no family names. Are they useless? The first names would be more important, but it is not up to me to reveal them to you. As for the family names, these apparently have the characteristic of not doubling any of their letters. [4] Their first names, on the other hand, have some relevance.

Unless the rite is stripped of its meaning—as Eucharist—when the fruits of the earth are appropriated by the male body. If meaning has indeed been twisted in this way, the whole horizon of Christianity would be perverse. The only interpretation of the earth man can make that would not take possession or evoke magic would be: we, men and women, are fruits of the earth and of our labor; in them, in us, among us, we commune, in the memory of Christ. The formula: "This is my body, this is my blood" that is pronounced over the bread and wine is in fact particularly unacceptable today when many celebrants and communicants care so little about the fate of the earth and its fruits and thus put the whole meaning of the eucharistic communion in doubt. Equally questionable is the appeal made in the mass to taste, as for example in the words of the consecration ("Take, eat ye all of this, this is my body . . ."), which are strongly reminiscent of the great spiritual traditions of India.

4. Or at least that was what the woman thought at first. This was probably her way of expressing her wish for a union innocent of all doubling. Details of this kind do not amount to an indiscretion, otherwise they would probably have set up a system of defenses operating through a kind of complicitous game. As for this text, its intent is to raise a veil from the scene of belief and the scene of truth—whence the allusion to proper names, for example. The woman's revelation may seem violent and sacrilegious to some people, both male and

So having this (*ça*) in poste restante, I read Jacques Derrida's *The Post Card*. Among other things in the book, I find—and this is the text that I will be concentrating on—the discussion of the *fort-da* of little Ernst. And, without any attempt to interpret as yet, I associated or joined the two scenes together. Are there not some obvious similarities between the two—notably Sophie, the Sunday daughter, whose death is so hard for her father to accept?

So, here is the *fort-da* scene as translated by Jacques Derrida:* "The child was not at all precocious in his intellectual development. At the age of one and a half he could say only a few comprehensible words; he could also make use of a number of sounds which expressed a meaning (*bedeutungsvolle Laute*, phonemes charged with meaning) to those around him. He was, however, on good terms with his parents and their one servant-girl, and tributes were paid to his being 'a good boy' (*anstandig*, easy, reasonable). He did not disturb his parents at night, he conscientiously obeyed orders not to touch certain things or go into certain rooms, and above all (*vor allem anderen*, before all else) he never cried when his mother left him for a few hours. At the same time, he was greatly attached to his mother, who had not only fed him herself but had looked after him without any outside help. This good little boy, however, had an occasional disturbing habit of taking any small objects he could get hold of and throwing them away from him into a corner, under the bed, and so on, so that hunting for (*Zusammensuchen*, looking for and collecting up) his toys (*Spielzeuges*) and picking them up was often quite a business" (*Postcard*, p. 307). As Jacques Derrida stresses, the famous reel or spool has not yet made its appearance. Here it comes now, preceded by an interpretative anticipation. "As he did this (as he threw away his *Spielzeug*) he gave vent to a loud, long-drawn-out 'o-

female. But without that revelation which reaches beyond the canonic enclosure of revelation, fidelity in history and confidence in certain of its figures become beliefs, dogmas, rites that are in part sacrificial and repressive. All this is not necessarily religious but seems essential to the establishment of priestly power over the people, a power that is handed down from father to son, to the exclusion of women, in our patriarchal tradition.

*The following passage consists of quotations from *Beyond the Pleasure Principle*, by Sigmund Freud (translated and edited by James Strachey, New York: Norton, 1961, pp. 8–9), with bracketed interpolations by Derrida. See *The Post Card: From Socrates to Freud and Beyond*, translated with an introduction and additional notes by Alan Bass (Chicago: University of Chicago Press, 1987). In his text, Bass has amended the Standard Edition translation to better match the French text used by Derrida. Most specifically, he has preferred the American word *spool* to the *reel* used by Strachey to translate *Spule*. I have kept the Strachey text intact.—Tr.

o-o-o', accompanied by an expression of interest and satisfaction. His mother and the writer of the present account were agreed in thinking (the daughter and the father, the mother and the grandfather are here conjoined in the same speculation) that this was not a mere interjection but represented the German word *fort* (gone, faraway). I eventually realized that it was a game and that the only use he made of any of his toys (*Spielsachen*) was to play 'gone' (*fortsein*) with them. One day I made the observation which confirmed my view. The child had a wooden reel (*Holzspule*) with a piece of string (*Bindfaden*) tied round it. It never occurred to him to pull it along the floor behind him, for instance, and play at its being a carriage. What he did was to hold the reel by the string and very skilfully (with great *Geschick*) throw it over the edge of his curtained cot (or veiled bed, *verhangten Bettschens*), so that it disappeared into it, at the same time expressing his expressive (*Bedeutungsvolles*) o-o-o-o. He then pulled the reel out of the cot again by the string and hailed its reappearance with a joyful *Da* (there). This, then, was the complete game (*komplette Spiel*)—disappearance and return (*Verschwinden und Wiederkommen*). As a rule one only witnessed its first act, which was repeated untiringly as a game in itself, though there is no doubt that the greater pleasure was attached to the second act" (*Postcard*, p. 309).

" 'This, then,' says Freud, 'was the complete game.' Which immediately implies: this, then, is the complete observation, and the complete interpretation of this game" (*Postcard*, p. 309).

"Instead of playing on the floor (*am Boden*), he insisted on putting the bed into the game, into play, on playing with the thing over the bed, and also in the bed. Not in the bed as the place where the child himself would be, for contrary to what the text and the translation have often led many to believe (and one would have to ask why), it appears he is not in the bed at the moment when he throws the spool. He throws it from outside the bed over its edge (*Rand*) from the other side, which quite simply might be into the sheets. And in any event, it is from "out of the bed" (*zog ... an dem Bett beraus*) that he pulls back the vehicle in order to make it come back: *da*. The bed, then is *fort*, which perhaps contravenes all desire, but perhaps not *fort* enough for the (grand)father who might have wished that Ernst had played more seriously on the floor (*am Boden*) without bothering himself with the bed. But for both of them, the distancing of the bed is worked upon by this *da* which divides and

shares it: too much or not enough. For the one or for the other"
(*Postcard*, p. 310).[5]

The mother's presence in the re-presentation presumes, therefore,
a rather white and transparent screen: air, canvas, veil. The curtain
or veil that covered the bed or the crib was white or very light in
color and probably was not wholly opaque. It's hard to imagine it
all black, absorbing the light, or a bright, glaring red or indeed any
color that would separate or confuse the two sides, the edges. The
child throws something over there, beyond, but not behind a wall or
behind a curtain that concealed, hid her, hid him definitively. Or at
least, that's what he believes. Neither he nor she really goes away or
disappears for good.

What Ernst wants is to master presence-absence with the help of
a more or less white, more or less transparent veil. Freud does not
seem to care about the nature or texture or indeed the color of this
veil. Apart from the thread and the reel he has nothing to say about
any of the things that ensure the return—how they are located in
reference to the child, the presence or absence in the room or the
house of the main actors in the play. He has nothing to say about
what properties in the veil make the going-return possible. That (*ça*)
has nothing to say to him—or not any more. Which is probably why
he is able to tell the story of this drama in all good conscience
without really knowing what he is telling or what he is talking
about. He is just pleased that his grandson, in all innocence, gives
him what he needs to go on writing his own text, his own life, both
their lives.

So Freud says nothing, knows nothing, wants to know nothing
about what stands between him and him, between him and her,
disappearing and reappearing in the scene with the reel, before
Ernst notices himself in the mirror. The veil is necessary as a setting,
a mediation for the performance of presence in absence, for the
process of re-presentation in this particular scene, where for the first

5. As I was rereading this text before including it in the collection *Sexes and Genealogies*,
I realized that I had always assumed that Ernst was playing with his own bed or crib, not
with the bed of his mother or his parents. Which explains why I took no notice of Derrida's
"into the sheets." My interpretation is an attempt to account for the constitution of the male
cultural subject in its philosophic and religious dimensions. The other scene would conjure
up, on the contrary, its at least partial other side or back side, through allusion to mother-
son incest. What is more, in my reading, it is not amazing that the bed should be *fort*. The
game occurs by day and children hate to stay in bed. On the other hand, they love to climb
out of bed when they like, especially if the bed is rather high and difficult to climb down
from. It seems to me that little Ernst's pleasure comes in part from this.

time the son plays symbolically with the mother, but it is then neglected, censored, repressed, forgotten by Freud. The father of psychoanalysis notes what it is that enables Ernst to confuse the other in himself, the other in the same, with a skill that surprises and amazes his grandfather, in particular through its topology (it occurs in front, not behind, for example): he takes note of it in his description, but then goes right on. What is the child throwing away from himself? Is it himself, her and him, him and her, her in him, him in her? These are questions Freud never pauses to ask. He too just moves on.

But he, after all, is not playing: he is framing a theory. This tale, in which the child's naïveté is useful as an objective, scientific guarantee, can be interpreted as he likes, thus standardizing, prescribing the desire of his descendants, indeed retroactively his own, and that of his ancestors. She must be thrown over there, put at a distance, beyond the horizon, so that she can come back to him, back inside him, so that he can take her back, over and over again, reassimilate her, and feel no sorrow. Freud simply notices the reel and the thread. A physical substitute for her (he says), an object, and a link that allows him to send her faraway, and bring her back to him, back inside him.

But does, in fact, the reel have anything to do with her? Or with him? With him, foetus, playing at going in and coming out of her with a cord, a placental-veil, a womb-bed, for example. This assumes that the disappearance-reappearance, inside-outside, outside-inside can be mastered, whereas in fact they can no more be mastered than the life-death watch that is our obligation from birth, if not before. This darling little boy believes that coming into the world or going out of it can be made into a game in this way. He *believes* it because it is not the truth. This is an event that can never be controlled or planned, obeying a necessity that can never be so easily played with. Except by killing, and fasting to death.

This game, too simple when related to her absence or presence, will undermine his language of beliefs. At the moment when he believes he is best able to master her appearance-disappearance, he is most slave to belief. Belief in himself and his power of course, but also in her, since his link to her depends upon the belief that she is there, when she is not, that she is there more when she is not there (here), that she is where she isn't. Once this split between the two has been achieved, everything is possible. The thread by which the son holds her/holds her back, and makes a game of her life-her death, their life-their death, opens up the way to any presence or absence, in or out of the world. The truth of the world plunges downward, opening up like a set of Chinese boxes. Anything can climb up or down, climb back up or down. The framework of desire of the child-king or god closes and opens the session, the play, or the world to any kind of appearance or disappearance. It authorizes the confusion or substitution of reality and unreality, truth and untruth, between something and nothing, someone and no one, a living person and a ghost, self and someone other, someone other and someone other again, someone other and someone same.

The most important *fort-da*—as you know, even, or especially when you refuse to believe it—refers, past the mother's presence, in the mother, beyond-veil, to the presence of God, beyond the sky, beyond the visual horizon. It moves away from the presence of the mother beyond veil, petticoats, pants, etc.—though this does not mean that the son does not send himself there in the first veil, the amniotic fluid and the placenta that separate him from the womb—away from the mother's presence, then, toward that of god beyond and in heaven. All the threads and all the sons (*tous les fils et les fils**) come and go between these two places of the invisible, those two hidden presences, between which everything is played out, in which everything meets. And what is being sent of hers, quite apart from the whole rigmarole of toys and objects, is not some phallus she guards jealously—even if this is a condition he depends on—but rather the mystery of a first crypt, a first and longed-for dwelling place, the happy time when he had a space in her, and she in him, when he owed his whole life to her, before any call or claim. He lives off her, feeds on her, is wrapped up in her, drinks her, consumes her, consummates her . . . before any call or claim. This is a gift that permits no mastery during its term, an infinite debt, an infused, diffuse, profuse, exhaustive presence, and he can play with it only at the cost of relegating her, by a qualitative leap, into some place beyond life and death. This life in turn becomes merely a kind of exodus between two paradises: the one split between biology and mythology or left in silence, and the other for which a certain knowledge claims to account. For these two places, there are therefore two different measures and transcriptions, or so it seems at least. It

---

* Play on the words *le fil*, thread, and *le fils*, son, both of which have the same plural, *les fils*.—Tr.

remains to be seen how the one is folded and bent into the other, as an immemorial store of fiction, of belief, that secretly underpins its truth.

During that time in her womb, then, haven of skin, of membranes, of water—a complete world, in fact, in which and through which he receives all he wants, with no need for work or clothing—air, warmth, food, blood, life, potentially even the risk of death, come to him via a hollow thread. Everything comes that route, without being called upon. To believe that she will always be there takes only a step or two at most. The hollow cord and the thread of the reel don't quite amount to the same thing. Once the primal bond is severed, she will be there only if he summons. But was she ever there?

Step number two, which comes before or after the first, and he thinks he can keep a hold on her by alternating between the two: she was there and was not there, she gave place yet had no place, except her womb, and even then. Within her womb, an amnion and a placenta, a whole world with its layers, its circuits, its vessels, its nourishing pathways, etc., a whole world of invisible relations that adheres to her womb, that takes place in her womb, that gives him pain and gives her pain when the time comes for her to push him out and be delivered. But this world is not to be confused with her. It is destroyed forever at birth and it is impossible ever to return to it. All kinds of veils may claim to take its place, seek to repeat it, but there can be no return to that first dwelling place.

In fact she was never there, except in that ceaseless transfusion of life that passed from her to him, by a hollow cord. She offers the possibility of entry into presence but has no place in it. No encounter is possible with her during the pregnancy.

The son, obviously, always wants to go back there. And, if he can't, doesn't he tear away bit by bit the whole membrane that separated him from her but created an inconceivable nearness that he can never cease to mourn? She is so close, invisibly penetrating him, and she remains an unmasterable presence, if such a word can still be used in this way for a relationship in which she flows into him and for him, without face or form.

The placenta is clearly the first veil that the child knows as his own. Yet, he seems to forget that it is his own, even if it is produced for him within her, even if she thereby gives herself to him asking nothing in return, and even if this first home is not without some

33

connection to her? The veil is his as much as hers, even if they share it. It stands between them, obviously: by its means she gives herself to him and within him.

But it seems that from now on he will impose the veil upon her much more than she on him. It is true that she has not begun to speak, that she has her place in the veil, that they have never really met each other face to face, as if their mouth-to-mouth, their mouth-to-ear were still mediated by an umbilicus. From his navel to his or their placenta and from the connection of that enveloping membrane to her womb, unconsciously there would continue to be a dialogue. This does not prevent him from wanting to master her, reduce her little by little to nothing, by constructing for himself all kinds of new enclosures, new homes, new houses, directions, dimensions, foods, in order to break the bond with her. Behind all these substitutes lies the belief that she stands, she stands there all-powerful.

Two steps, then. The string of the reel is *not* like the first cord and does *not* bring her to him: he merely believes this and weaves this absence into his language. And, what is more, she should *not* simply be equated with the first dwelling place. To have access to her—to woman—would come after the nostalgia for this return into her, for that move back into the lost paradise where she shelters him and feeds him with and through her/their container. To have access to her demands another threshold than the one where she always stands behind the veil. The veil has served the life they once shared and can never be repeated. Later, it serves as a hideout or hiding place for all or nothing. In this game of hide and seek, the son plays with himself alone: with him in her, her in him, before any meeting face to face can occur. The game takes the place of that encounter, takes over from it, overtakes and overcomes it, weaving a whole world, from the depths of the earth to the highest heavens. Everything is set up in such a way that she is lost at the poste restante, never arrives at the destination, never comes face to face with him. This encounter between them can perhaps take place only in the form of a scar, a wound that he reopens in her, or fears truly to reopen, in order to close himself off. He opens the wound in her womb so that he can close up his navel, his heart, or his mouth over the wound left by her absence, her disappearance from him. This requires a whole game with his geometry, both Euclidian and more advanced, his vectorizations of space: horizontal and vertical, strings and veils, which exist only because she is faraway and because he believes that, when he sent her far off like this, she will come back the same, whereas she returns to the other in the same (*le même*). This difference undermines the truth of his language: a credulousness is introduced in the power of the subject that thereby constitutes itself, plays even as it is played with. He remains eternally in exodus from the place that transcends all that in which he might at last discover the truth of truth, in some ontological or theological heaven. The two are not unrelated, maintain their mutual situation, control what takes place, and what does not. Here too there is no lack of flights and soaring.

For all this to succeed, a more or less transparent veil was needed that ensures a certain number of passages between him and her within representation, a certain number of repetitions in which he believes he masters the mother, completely. In the scene as he sets it up, he stands in the middle, where the string-cord begins. She would come back to the middle. And, if he can only pivot around a little, always looking straight on, or, straight on but all around, he thus reconstructs—he believes—his first dwelling place.

And, as all this remains very much on the primary level, very loose even if all the strings are already in place, before he buckles it all up, closes or sutures the ways in and out, space itself is still capable of expanding almost infinitely, a cosmogony is possible in which the unconscious (*ça*) moves on, stretches, propagates, travels at lightning speed. So before the son has perfected his stage set, one can try and steal his veil away from him, take the curtain of his theater, the means or mediator of his *fort-da*, and loan it or give it back to the *angels*.

The veil that ludically separates him from her, from himself, from himself in her, from her in himself, this veil that will divide off and surround his drama, evokes or perhaps recalls something of the angel. Angels have been as misunderstood, forgotten, as the nature of that first veil, except in the work of poets, perhaps, and in religious iconography.

Yet the whiteness of angels, their semitransparence, their lightness, the question of their sex, their purity (in the Rilkean sense: as pure as animals), could all these attributes not be a reappearance or recollection of that by which and thanks to which messages from the beyond are transmitted? Beyond what? The ultimate veil. Whence they would emerge. Always coming from beyond the horizon. And yet the element traversed would not be opaque or very colored, but rather airy, allowing free passage—like the angel. Who is sent, or comes, from heaven, on a mission, to do a job. In fact the angel always returns to heaven, goes home, to the other side of the ultimate veil. Unless he stands there, if only for a fragment, a flight, a detached soar that is sent, addressed, to announce what comes after. Awesome call or recall that circulates so swiftly and lightly, an annunciation of more weight than any coded message, moving to and fro between the first and last dwellings that are withheld from present visibility or readability, to be deciphered only in the next world. From beyond the angel returns with inaudible or unheard of words in the here and now. Like an inscription written in invisible ink on a fragment of body, skin, membrane, veil, colorless and unreadable until it interacts with the right substance, the matching body.

We have to search back very far to find it, assuming it (*ça*) can be found, far beyond and deep within the language, in its first bed or nest or cradle of beliefs. There, always undecipherable and undeciphered, unless one passes-passes back through God and his angels, bent and folded up within every message and every code, forming the basis for every potential inscription, is this *veil*, through which there once took place and perhaps will again take place the sympathy between two bodies capable of mutually decoding one another. We shall need to go as far as the last veil and beyond if, one day, this (*ça*) is to pass back, through him, between him and her, her and him, not by means of some regressive return to a place that is lost forever nor in a completely other place from which that first place would be relegated for good.

While we wait for this to happen—assuming it can, or hasn't already, though not face-to-face—this sympathetic deciphering of bodies, skins, membranes, mucuses, while we are waiting then, sometimes a mediating angel or angels come to give us news about the place where the divine presence may be found, speaking of the word made flesh, returning, awaited.

The angels come down and go up, go up and come down in a vertical mediation, like that of the veil over the stage, which they claim is primary, and which, on this occasion, would go from highest to lowest, a structure permitting the movement to and fro, back and forth from heaven to earth, going from one to the other through the various containing layers, but upon which, apparently, *nothing is inscribed.*

If my children's story is applied to Ernst, the angel who helps him while his mother is gone is a good angel. There are, as you know, the bad angels, who want to become like God, who block the mediating channels, stand in the path of movement to and fro, back and forth. In this case, the stand-in angel seems good, at least as far as Ernst and his grandfather are concerned. Perhaps not for her since she ends up excluded from the party, sent away, for good in the end. The angel in this case is rather under the thumb of the child-king or god, even of his grandfather. The angel is interposed to allow and preserve or to allow the preservation of the relationship, the rapport. He seems to be in the service of the son as well as of the string and the reel that is thrown away and pulled back, far or near Ernst. There seems to be only one angel, who obeys the son, and perhaps the grandfather: the mother's father. She seems to have no angel. She is thrown away and pulled back by means of the angel, but she herself cannot use that mediation, that messenger. She fulfills the desire or the word of the child-god, and previously of her father, but sends no message of her own. She yields to his call, yields to being called back, thrown away—far from herself or from him—then brought back into him, beyond any veil. The angel even stands in the way between God and herself so that she can be sent away from the men and can come back outside herself, in him, in them, between them.

Does she stay the same once she has been thrown away, put at a distance, pulled back, brought near, in this way? No. On her return, he has wrapped her in his own veil, his own call, his, or their—the men's—own language. He has taken possession of the veil or canvas that traces the limits of his desire, his will, his pleasure, and, now, he plays with it. She will always be there, she will always be in, when he wants. He will only have to call her, call her back, and she will be re-present(ed) to him, in his world.

This protects him from disappearing into her. This return annihilates that other return that might swallow him up, take him back into that first dwelling place inside her. And anytime he comes near her he will be armed with this little toy: a reel with a more or less elastic string, a veil over her but also a mask (a phallic mask, for example) that shrouds his own reel. This invisible supplement to the body helps in time of danger, rather like a guardian angel—which may be something of a devil[6]—that he dispatches before sending any message. Mediation of the message before any message exists, it is the condition of representation and presentation. Always placed between presence and absence, if, in this case, this pairing has any meaning. But perhaps it has meaning only in this case.

So the angel dispatches himself, or receives himself, or listens to himself, earlier than any conception, birth, flight to heaven or back to heaven. *Even before the hymen* the angel makes the annunciation. Unless he takes the place of the hymen, unless he comes to its assistance from somewhere outside place, outside the game, as is generally believed. Everything, it seems, happens earlier, in a word in which something of the first veil is brought back in the name of God and the engendering of the son. Mysteriously, she seems to receive through her ear all that has been taken away from her womb. Structure bearing the message but not its inscription, related to the sense of hearing without any need for skin or membrane to be broken or perforated. A great deal of sympathy is needed to decipher this, to unveil the secret of the game.

But does a complete unveiling occur? Or does this merely announce, prefigure, is it just the expectation of a resurrection, an ascension, a return? How are we to know if the angel is coming from beyond the ultimate veil or if he is simply announcing this coming? If the one who is expected is coming back again for some early encounter or is coming at last? If we are dealing here with a prologue or the fulfillment of presence? Or again: if what the angel does and says is the work of a ghost, sent back from the beyond to haunt us. Beyond what? And how are life and death to be kept apart in this case?

Could it be that this risk of assimilating life into death occurs because of the angel's one-way journey? The angel always goes in the same direction, even on his two-way trips: from heaven where the God-Father is supposed to be, to her, for example, with the mission of giving or entrusting her with his offspring. But isn't this all rather twisted around? When the angel goes toward her, might he not actually actually be coming from her? Hasn't the angel taken off from her, flown away from her? Skin and membrane that can

---

6. This is one way of understanding that all phallic norms make sexuality devilish in the sense that this order is interposed to blur the sympathy between the sexes.

hardly be perceived, almost transparent whiteness, almost undecipherable mediation, which is always at work in every operation of
language and representation, ensuring that the lowest earth and
highest heaven are linked, that first dwelling place in her, from
which he makes and remakes his bed, and works out the transcendence of the Lord.

Doesn't the angel announce, in some way, that she is also an angel
and that she will bring an angel into the world? A couple that will
give rise to a new conception of the flesh, to those miracles owed to
touch, with or without words, that we know as transfiguration, resurrection, ascension, or assumption? A couple of angels or in which
all angels would concentrate their function as mediators—and beyond? But this couple does not appear as such, or at least not according to canonical revelation. She remains only mother and he son,
the two obedient to the words of the Father. And when the angel
announces the news to her, brings her the message, he already comes
or comes back from God the Father. The veil and the reel, it seems,
can be given back to her only through Him, after the mediation of
his writing. Her duty is to remain the supporting structure that
permits absence to be separated from presence in re-presentation.
This substrate would be her property, or at least her lot, but the son
seems to have taken it over, and the father with him, and it would
come back to her only if moved by an Other, the All High, omnipo-
tent Father, center and matrix of reference for all our beliefs.

The angel is terrible, terrifying, as Rilke says. He reminds us of
something that is meant to be eternally forgotten. He conjures up
something that has not been written legibly, with a word that moves
through it without stopping, but without which she would not be
that which can give place to the presence she has in his re-presentation.

But there also are the *devils*. These are not angels, who go and
come from high to low, mediators for heaven and earth in their airy
journeys across all frontiers, creatures of flight and soar, breath,
veils, wings, airs, unfettered by allegiance to port or shore. Who
make themselves known in cryptic messages, oracles, dreams. Who
come to meet us openly, face-to-face, even if in confrontation or
opposition.

The devils, on the other hand, don't work as discreet mediators.
Their job is to disrupt and to confuse. They block mediation, blur its
message, burn it sometimes, before it can be heard and heeded.

Perhaps they were merely angels before the fall. But, by wishing to be like or more than the angels, and, ultimately, like and more than God, they ceaselessly cut and disrupt the path leading into presence. Their wish to be *like* means to wish always to be more than, to take over the place or the post and give them more power. By wishing always and still to outdo, overcome, they double the angels, and, ultimately, God, by claiming to intercept or turn the veil, fraying the barely perceptible thread of communication. They never stop crossing mediation with their doublings, mimes, interventions by means of an other yet like force that is quantitatively greater. They block the way by repeating, even within themselves, the circuit of transfer (of life and of death, of assimilation and disassimilation). They confuse ancestors and descendents, push genealogy off track, jumble communication, break communion. In their darkness they capture and make a screen against any transmission of light and send none back. They are seen or make more of an impact more often even though they are, or because they are, negatives. But the negatives of a positive that exists before any printed image, any fixed representation, immobilizing or blurring the call to or expectation of any possibility of presence. Perhaps they are the negatives of angels, easy to draw but difficult to photograph, given their relation to light. Angels can only be approached with extreme sympathy, great intimacy. The diabolic, on the other hand, would be an effect of overexposure or underexposure because it wills to double the other. It operates by blocking the attraction of presence—which can be perceived but yet not defined—and those gestures and words that announce it explicitly or succeed in making it flesh. The devil gets in the way. He blocks understanding, sets the stage by paralyzing it through a mimicry that turns it upside down, reproduces it in many copies, backwards: back/front, up/down, etc. In this way he rubs out one faint trail and blazes another. Ultimately, in the representation of history, we will remember him alone, even as we believe we are perpetuating the memory of the angel—and beyond—of all that the angel brings and sends back. But the angel mediates by keeping space open and marking the trail from the oldest of days to the farthest future of the world. Serving as active memory, even if it remains unconscious, this mediation is turned by the diabolical will to reproduce the relation to light into an inscription that makes the rules, or at times into a writing that hides the source.

There's only one chance: the angel goes before the devil. He takes place earlier. If one can manage to clear a way past the devil's obstructive workings, sometimes one comes upon this awesome destiny, this daunting encounter. Otherwise, the whole stage is taken over by the devil, the devils, who turn everything upside down to make the leap and make us leap into dark, hidden, sulfurous beyond. Unless the whole thing goes suddenly up in flames? Otherwise, the future endlessly recycles the past, after assimilation and disassimilation that blinds the eyes.

The devil's work blinkers us, allowing us to see only itself, blocks any movement to and fro from past to future, traps us, stymies us, leads us round and about into a dead end. (Unless we yield to him wholly, pass completely over to the devil?) He blurs the future and any hint we may receive of it. He closes the frame to keep out light and air: he is only to be seen, even though he never appears. But he is there, already and forever dark. In our encounters, from now on, each of us, man and woman, meets only his or her image. Only doubles are present and represented, only reproductions, kinds of negatives, reduced prints—only the angel can give light and expansion. In encounters like these, no hint of the future remains. Everything seems to be programmed, predictable. All that remains is to pursue this strange continuum, series. Unless, perhaps, an essential difference befalls us.

It is true that there is some use in standing back, taking things only in retrospect, for someone who wanders in the heavens or drowns in the depths, who is overwhelmed by the immensity of time and space with no partitions, no possible demarcations, no people or objects to play with, no distance that can be mastered with a reel and a string.

So the answer is to use the other as a screen. Position the other in front of the heavens and the deep chasms, and look only at what the other has already been able to assimilate-disassimilate. While the other is framing and being framed in this way, the man who stands behind this device, this telesetup, can relax a bit. Nothing need be predicted for the moment of his own history, his own goals, his own moves. He analyzes a posteriori, sheltered by the *fort-da* from all that precedes him, from his body, or his flesh.

But why the devil—we may aptly exclaim—does Plato-the-son stand behind Socrates?[7] Why does the son, or sons, stand behind the (spiritual) fathers and not the mothers, given that the sons are really

---

7. See in this regard Jacques Derrida's *Postcard.*

41

trying to possess the mothers? If we are to reframe the paternal scenario, see how it made its mark, play it backward, we cannot merely master the female whom the father was always seeking to take or take back in his threads, the female who, already, exceeded the father and whom he endlessly sought to bring back into his game. The son merely listens attentively to the father's game (or sometimes vice versa), tests out how he came to situate her, and to situate himself, within her and in relation to her. In order to learn in what history of hers he has been taken and has taken her, the son takes the measure of the father's game, intends to take him by surprise, take him by surprise in the figures of the game, their placings and enlacings. He is not encountering *her* but the father who encounters her, the father's links to her, his place in relation to her, his place as it issues from and with her. By this retroaction the son gives himself or gives himself back, with or without her, a *face* that can be present, rediscovered, behind the father's back. Equally, he gives himself or gives himself back a volume by moving around the father. But why not around her? Because she can only be encountered piece by piece, step by step. But if he arrived at the limits of known spatiality he would lose his favorite game, the game of mastering her.

There is another way of refusing or rejecting the angel, or angels, another way of not hearing the message, or distorting its direction and dimension: this is to deprive the mediator of his word, his presence, and blindly and cynically to implant it or anchor it in another site, another earth or heaven than the one it came from originally. Thus, seeking to capture the angel in the home, any home— be it house, hostel, temple, altar—and covering what lives there in the guise of the messenger is another kind of diabolic paralysis that freezes movements and words. To seek to cage up within the domestic setting something that has always flowed uncontained is like turning free soaring, rapture, flight into parchments, skeletons, death masks.

If we do not rethink and rebuild the whole scene of representation, the angels will never find a home, never stay anywhere. Guardians of free passage, they cannot be captured, domesticated, even if our purpose is to see ourselves in them. They can light up our sight and all our senses but only if we note the moment when they pass by, hear their word and fulfill it, without seeking to show, demonstrate, prove, argue about their coming, their speaking, or appearance. Without trying somehow to keep them at our disposal, in a transfer of destination that obscures and befuddles everything: with no face or name corresponding anymore to the angel's place or his light, his faith or his truth.

This game that we play with the angel's whiteness and transparence, this claim that all things are equal in appearance, this crazy, demented gaze that reduces a multiplicity of objects, or at least two, to one perfect resemblance, surrounding them with that which makes matter out of form for each man or woman, and their spatiality, this game is certainly the most diabolic temptation that exists. This is how the veil and the angel are appropriated and destroyed, leaving the air empty of loving leadership.

The angel always engages with us face-to-face, even if it is to affront or to assail. Unlike devils and animals or at least the mammals who are our nearest relatives and who engage from behind, the angel returns in front, stands in front. But when he comes to us, returns to us in this way, he is often alone. If he is calling us and recalling us to some lost encounter, face-to-face, he is alone as he gives his message.

Except in the Holy of Holies? Behind the temple veil. Then there are two of them. There the angels face one another over the ark of the covenant, standing at the two ends of the mercy seat of which they make one piece. The mercy seat *covers* the ark, can be detached from it, and serves in atonement, in washing away sin. It is in this place that Yahweh appears to Moses and speaks to him from between the cherubim.

In Exodus 26, verses 17 to 22, Yahweh speaks to Moses and says: "And thou shalt make a mercy seat of pure gold: two cubits and a half shall be the length thereof, and a cubit and a half the breadth thereof. And then thou shalt make two cherubim of gold, of beaten work shalt thou make them, at the two ends of the mercy seat. And make one cherub at the one end, and one cherub at the other end: of one piece with the mercy seat shall ye make the cherubim on the two ends thereof. And the cherubim shall spread out their wings, with their faces one to another; toward the mercy seat shall the faces of the cherubim be. And thou shalt put the mercy seat above upon the ark; and in the ark thou shalt put the testimony that I shall give thee. And there I will meet with thee, and I will commune with thee from above the mercy seat, from between the two cherubim which are upon the ark of the testimony, of all things which I will give in commandment unto the children of Israel."*

So here, two angels face one another to guard the presence of God, who may perhaps be turning away in his anger or absence. The angels face one another over the ark of the covenant. Beneath them, the tablets of the law, and between them, between their wings, the divine presence that cannot be sensed or seen. The doubling of the angel (and of the veil? You know that the veil of the temple covering the entrance to the Holy of Holies will be rent when the Son of Man dies, meaning also the coming of his resurrection) would keep Yahweh from being closed up in the text of the law. It seems to be setting up the future presence of God in the more airy element: he can come and go freely, the word that has already been offered and inscribed in stone is loosed, and a new covenant is prepared.

Two angels who face one another—this event could only take place here. They turn toward one another, guarding and calling the divine presence between them. They do not go in one single direction. There are two of them, halted in their paths. Face-to-face, they stand in almost timid contemplation, intent on something that has yet to come, yet to be situated, not yet inscribed, written, spoken. They shelter what may take place because they are two and are turned toward one another. Coming from opposite directions, to meet one another, they halt the return from sameness to sameness, before any determination or opposition of presence or absence can be made. Here is there no course taken, no reel, no string, no mastery of re-presentation? They are turned toward, or—one might imagine—turned away from, according to what they are guarding or are no longer guarding. Face-to-face or back to back.

Are the two alike? We might believe so. But those who are alike tend to engage with each other from the back, moving step by step, in single file, the one taking the other's place, supplanting him or possessing him in his place, so as to move forward. Those who are different are more likely to face one another, except as animals, at least according to the most pregnant imaginary. So, is it true to say that like beings place themselves to the rear, unless some idealiza-

* Later English translations use the expression "ark of the tokens" rather than "ark of the covenant" or "ark of the testimony," and refer simply to a "cover" over the ark, rather than a propitiatory or mercy seat.—Tr.

tion is already at work—in the mirror? squared?—whereas different beings stand face-to-face, except in the transgression of the matrix of idealization?

Those angels, perhaps, heed none of these imperatives. Neither like nor other, they guard and await the mystery of a divine presence that has yet to be made flesh. Alike and different, they face each other, near enough and far enough for the future to still be on hold. Neither God, nor men nor women, nor beasts, nor language seem yet to have found their final destiny. Neither God, nor difference of the sexes, nor difference between man and animal seem decided upon once and for all, already really made flesh.

Something lives there out of site, or perhaps between sites, some airy, mobile and yet material structure serving to bear presence, for the one, for the other, and for the unique in this relationship, of this relationship.

Something, forever deferred until the divine comes or comes back, perhaps has never taken place in this advent setup between the two angels: the advent of flesh itself, which in its most airy, subtle rapture might go beyond or before a certain sexual difference, once that difference has first been respected and fulfilled.

Beyond and before this parting of ways, enveloping it as its future advent and ultimate home, here stand the angels in deep meditation. At least two of them, facing, close, just far enough apart to prevent the uncountable touch of the flesh from blending into contact with the two ends. Between them the flesh holds back and flows forth before any mastery can be exercised over it, or after a *fort-da* far more sophisticated than the reel, a *fort-da* of the possibility of presence and of sharing in something divine that cannot be seen but can be felt, underlying all incarnation, which two angels, facing but not looking at each other, set up between them.

My conclusion would be that if tradition says nothing about their sex, it is because they are of a different sex and because tradition knows nothing of sexual difference. So it must be if the flesh of God is to become flesh. Tradition does say that (*ça*), but without wanting to make any statements about the sex of the angels—who have yet to experience any sexual engagement.

Besides, the angels of the ark of the covenant are neither human nor animals. Sphinxes each of them, each for the other? they wait, and wait for each other. Lacking not the lure but the threshold of the entry into presence.

This threshold appears to be blocked, notably in the myth of Aristophanes in the *Symposium*, if I need to give an example. The yoking of two into one same one paralyzes the whole scene. There is no space between him and her, between the men and the women. Unless it be a diagonic space? A kind of match that has been squared *into sameness*, played out obliquely to closed stations. The stage is loaded with blurred shapes, blocked movements, duels for dominance. Whatever the struggle, no future is possible. Memory does not go back far enough. Or rather it returns home to master the other, without making any motion to go beyond.

But, in such a permutuation between, what remains to be achieved of the one and of the other? Unless the permutations are merely apparent, possible only because each remains what he or she was, for fear of flying off into envelopes that are lacking in all resources? Only death lies on this path, no interpenetration of different germ cells is now possible. The statue is fixed forever into a figure that equates one sex to the other, without any relationships between them henceforth, no possible creation or rejuvenation.

Thus the body that gives life never enters into language. Ernst, the son, believes perhaps that, in his first language game, he holds his mother. She has no place there. She subsists before language as the woman who gives her flesh and her blood, and beyond language as she who is stripped of a matrix/womb, a veil, an enclosure or a clearing in which she might live according to the horizon of her games, symbolizations, representations. She remains the elemental substrate of life, existing before all forms, all limit, all skin, and of heaven, visible beyond-horizon. Between these extremes stand the angels and the annunciation of the fulfillment of the flesh.

In the meantime, the stake in the game is split between him and her. Both of them bleeding, the one openly, the other secretly, but he and she remain bound to their functions as son and mother. Yet he puts her at a distance, seeking the society of the father. Together he and the father organize the world, bless the fruits of the earth, identify them with their body and blood, and in this way effect the communion between the units of the people that have been neutered, at least apparently. In effect, the women in attendance must be mothers, mothers of sons, whereas *the other*, the woman lover, is kept away from the scene. No one must see that it is they, the wives and mothers, who are being offered up in communion here, who effect the communion, that, like the earth and its fruits, it is the

body and the blood especially of virgin women that are being sacri-
fied to that intermale society. The duty to bear children, to be silent,
to be in attendance but off on the side—all this wounds the flesh and
the spirit of women, and there is no representation of that sacrifice.
In fact, it is doubled in the duty women have to believe and to be
practicing believers. Dogmas and rites appear as substitutions and
veils that hide the fact that women's carnal and spiritual virginity
is being sacrificed and traded. The sons are separated from their
mothers and from the women who love them out of duty to their
Fathers.

But who is the Father if his will is that flesh be abolished? Is this
the meaning of religion, as some would have us believe? Or are we
dealing with the crypt of an order set up by one sex that claims to
write the rules of truth at the price of life? Henceforth, are the sons
not obliged to play weird games of *fort-da* between mothers who are
by some extraordinary turn virgins and fathers who are mysteriously absent? How are the spirit and mind to be woven of the
threads of remoteness, belief, paralysis, denial, and negation of
life?

This is how men gather together in the mystery of the here and
now present of a body and a blood that have not figured on the stage
and thus allow that stage to be set. Many, many years ago, in our
tradition, the pick was driven into the earth-mother's womb in order
to build the sacred enclosure of the tribe, the temple, finally the
house.

But there are still flowers, since after all we still feel a need to
spend a little time on earth, in the sunshine, to open up to the joy of
light and air, to pulse to the rhythm of the seasons. There are roses,
if I may evoke the flower that, despite its thorns, has so often been
celebrated by poets, philosophers, and divines. Mysteriously, the
rose's bloom recalls something of blood and of the angel. It is reborn
ceaselessly, causelessly, because it must bloom, having no care for
itself, no need to be seen, following in its own cycle and the cycle of
the world. The flower is like a pure apparition of natural generation,
the angel is like a pure vector of spiritual spatiality, rapt purity
before any conception occurs, any meeting of fixed dimensions or
directions.

There is the rose, before and after the bloom, forever opening for
the first and last time. And yet the arrangement of its petals knows
all the roses that have been and are to come, but with no doubles, no

replicas. Even as the rose opens up, it already knows about shedding petals, dying down, lying dormant, not as an end but as a recovery. Except for the petals surrounding or cradling the heart—those at the very center—the rose's petals are grouped front against back (or the opposite, depending on the presentation), in against out, with inside protecting outside. By thus pursing the lips that have already been opened, offered, the flower seems to guard against dispersion, in a movement contrasting with that of the son who keeps throwing away his many toys or, on each occasion, his woman-mother, either whole or in torn fragments. Sorrow and loss will accompany his memory as it seeks to shelter the inside from an overwhelming outside by clothing and closing itself in with roof, house, appearances. This may deceive him, lead him into error or temptation as to what goes to the heart, the inmost center, or the source. The rose within itself—if we can speak in this way—seems imperceptibly veiled by its repose in or about an invisible composure. Its inmost secret calyx is never shown, it lies beneath all the gathered petals. When the petals have opened completely in immodest splendor, the place in which the rose once touched herself, lip to lip, has disappeared. You will never see it. You will never see what she is or has in her heart of hearts. Perhaps it—or he? or she?—can be sensed by someone living close to the rose, breathing the space around her, which she creates with that caress in which she subsists freely offering herself, in a gift that wafts through the air unseen, untouched. But so easy to lose.

The heart of the rose opens without the need of a blueprint. In the heart of a flower there is nothing—but the heart. It opens for no reason. No teleology directs the petals to unfurl. They serve no function. Unless it is to be gazed upon? But what gaze? The rose looks at us from somewhere where it is not represented. A calendar for the world, the rose recalls sight to a presence virgin of mastery, to a gaze still innocent of all manufactured and reproducible presence. In a certain sense it is invisible, while being so much more visible than anything that is represented. It is neither object nor thing. It cannot speak itself in words, even though a certain set of syllables designate the rose in our language. It has no double. It always gives itself for the first unique time. It draws our eyes in its contemplation, arrests them—for no reason. Our gaze opens—for no reason, bathed in its blossoming.

Movements without forces. Features determined without the rigid requirement to apply some kind of energy. Petals without firm shapes. In-finite finitude, unlimited. Splendor of imperfection.

What is offered in this way is the very movement of blossoming, a growth that is not entrusted merely to the veiling-unveiling activity of the gaze but allows itself to be seen as it blooms. The *phuein* seems to escape the eye, which counts upon itself alone. *Upokeimenon* that is perceived only when complete, leaving in the shadow all that contributes to the availability of what is offered to the gaze.

In the movement of the *proteron te phusei* may be found the heart of thought, that which remains veiled in what thought says and which speaking obeys as some secret command. But already, when it speaks, thought no longer speaks what moves it. It no longer retains that emotion even as a fault in speech, as a dark night out of which it would expect to burst forth. Thought excludes the heart that moves it. That which makes thought live is spoiled, set outside of it. But it does not know this. Like a firm foundation that itself has no foundation upon which it would rely calmly, careless of the distress rising from the abyss.

As long as it does not touch upon that abyss, thought can still breathe. But it runs out of breath and food and takes no notice. And the sublime, which thought consumes, is transformed into utilities. Instead of singing the lost trace of vanished gods—the sacred ether that it leaves in the night—thought dismembers this being (*étant*) that is no being at all but shelters the mystery of every being. It shreds the air to coin it into values, trumpery values that no longer even shine with that mysterious light of being (*être*). Those garments, which can always be changed, no longer clothe any person in their own radiance, but are loaned out, substituted, calculated to function as a kind of pleasing that masks nothingness but not abandonment. Exercises in futility torn from the poet's flesh that has been left in distress, at the heart of all that oblivion allows, still, to appear. The poet alone remembers the bond that ties men and gods, recalls the nonappearance of the air in which some trace of the sacred remains. He questions, over and over, that presence which does not show itself and yet persists, as a shelter, in time of want, for all that resists calculation. Love, pain, life and death, are kept there, secret, enigmatic, barely breathing out their melody beyond or through all speakable words.

But can a mortal still sing? And how to speak of his song? Has the quarrel between the poet and the thinker already gone far enough to make a basis for their agreement? This will not occur without risk.

A risk that risks life itself, going beyond it barely by a breath.[8] A breath that, if it is held, saves through song, prophet of pure forces that call out and refuse shelter. Does not everything already in existence paralyze the breath? Imperceptibly occupying the air, preventing its free use, strangling with multiple coils anything still anxious to cross this captive atmosphere.

And anyone who does not go down into the abyss can only repeat and retrace the ways already opened that cover over the trace of the vanished gods. Alone, always alone, the poet runs the risk of moving outside the world and turning over what it opens up until touching the bottom of the bottomless, saying yes to something calling him from beyond the horizon. As he stands abandoned, he retains at most a breath, that first and final energy forgotten until it fails. Everywhere present, yet invisible, it grants life to everything and everyone, on pain of death. Risk taken at each moment by the poet, that seeker after the still sacred ether, which today is so covered over or buried that he can trust no heaven or earth, learn his path from no mouth, find no sure direction. For him no place is habitable, since his mission is to reopen a ferial site. Thus he has to leave the world, while yet remaining mortal, go off to some shore that bears no signpost, to love a life assured by none. To achieve this he has no firm ground. He must tear himself away from his native land to plunge his roots into a ground that is virgin, unknown, unpredictable. Free for risk.

He even lets go of that captivating magic that makes men kin to each other, becomes an exile from any will belonging to an existing community, descending into the hell of history to seek traces of life there, seeds still held in unturned subsoil. Seeds to set free, to lay in the air even though they may produce something that has never yet appeared, may give rise to a new blossoming, stripped of protection, of shelter, of home. No veil? To advance into danger is to lay the self bare before any answering confidence has been granted. Here, there is no betrothal, no site. Terror becomes consent to every-

---

8. Following the Cerisy conference in August 1980, these last pages were used in somewhat modified form in my book, *L'oubli de l'air chez Martin Heidegger* (Paris: Edition de Minuit, 1982). Sometimes this section echoes the essay "Why Poets?" in Heidegger's *Poetry, Language, Thought* (translated by A. Hofstadter, New York: Harper and Row, 1971).

thing, permission for everything that touches, without refusal or withdrawal.

Risk protects anyone who, insensibly, invisibly, moves onward while remaining in his own heart. Who is still alien to existence as one who yields, offers himself freely to the other outside himself and receives himself back in return. Access to a space and a time whose dimensions surpass the stars as well as the imaginary of each conscience. Objective and subjective lose their limits thereby. Each person and all things rest in one another, flow one into the other unconfined. Recollection of a state so ancient that few are capable of it. Crossing the frontiers of their own lives, following far and near, risking their breath, they yield the very rhythm of their breath to the other, agreeing to lose the beat of their pulse in order to discover a new amplitude. In this way they expire one into the other, and rise up again inspired. Imperiling that citadel of being, language, so that this woman, that man, can find a voice, a song.

Leaving a temple already consecrated, they seek the traces of the ferial bond with the wholly other being. No longer having words, risking speech itself, they have no anxiety because nothing is calculated, they are strangers to exchange, business, marketplace. They tremble at the coming of that which has been announced, that other breath born to them after all known resonance has been broken, beyond everything that has already been achieved. Beyond the unheard sonority of the watchers who do not venture out into the infinite journey of the invisible. The only guide here is the call to the other, whose breath subtly impregnates the air like a vibration perceptible to these men lost for love. They go on, attentively, boldly moving forward over paths where others see only shadows and hell. They move forward, and at times a song comes to their lips. From their mouths issue sounds that have no meaning—only the inspiration that will strike the other with the feelings and thoughts that overwhelm them. Responses, mostly inaudible, to what they sense in the wind. They breathe confidently, carefree because they lack the anxiety of their security. They have willed to strip away all structure and rely only upon the attraction they perceive that pulls them beyond all frontiers. They agree to walk where they are borne, as far as the source that gives them themselves, unreservedly attaining all that draws them on and letting it flow out again in the fullness of the gift. In this movement to and fro no dwelling has been built, no shelter set up. This consent and its reward take place without additional protection for those who risk their lives in this way. They do not end up in some enclosure that guarantees they will come to no harm, they are not separated. In rapturous consent, they receive and give themselves in the open.

The way to this strange adventure is found in the renunciation of any path that has already been proposed. Anything that once offered a possible future must be abandoned, turned back, like a limited horizon: a veil that imperceptibly conceals the world facing us. Before the departure, all goals must at the very least be turned upside down, every plan must be upset. Those who dare all make their way without maps as blind men do. Free of the spell that made them afraid to be without a shelter, they yield unrestrainedly to the open, a place where men free from fear can embrace and blossom. Offering every aspect of themselves to straight scrutiny, joining their forces, acting upon one another in the integrity of a perception that has no refusal in the center of its pure gravity, they say yes, unreservedly, to the whole of the experience to come.

Even to death, as one other face of life? Yes. And to the other as other? Yes? Or is it still a matter of remaining in one's own realm? While accepting the reverse, of course, making the negative a positive, naturally, but always acting in the same way. Once the sphere of application has been extended, there enters into it something that shapes a horizon that turns back into a vast imperceptible film whose outside is endlessly given within, unveiling and reveiling what has been closed up in one site.

Beyond go one to the other those who give up their own will. Beneath every speech made, every word spoken, every point articulated, every rhythm beaten out, they are drawn into the mystery of a word that seeks incarnation. While trusting beyond measure in that which gives flesh to speech: air, breath, song, they reciprocally receive and give something that is still crazy, and are thereby reborn by giving each other the gift of a speech of forgotten inspiration, buried beneath logic and indeed beneath all existing language. This suspension of all meaning unveils the commerce that underlies meaning, and risks going back to a time when separation had not yet occurred, when there was as yet no attempt to rate this as more valuable than that. In this opacity, this night of the world, they discover the trace of vanished gods, at the very point when they have given up their safety. Light shines on them once they have agreed that nothing shall ensure their protection, not even that age-old citadel of man—being (*être*)—not even that guarantor of the meaning or nonmeaning of the world—God.

These prophets know that if anything divine is still to come our way it will be won by abandoning all control, all language, and all sense already produced, it is through risk, only risk, leading no one knows where, announcing who knows what future, secretly commemorating who knows what past. No project here. Only this refusal to refuse what has been perceived, whatever distress or wretchedness may come of it.

These predecessors have no future, They come from the future. In them it is already present. But who hears it? Silently their song irrigates the world of today, of tomorrow, of yesterday. The need for this destiny is never heard clearly, never appears in broad daylight without suffering disfigurement.

But the breath of one who sings while mingling his inspiration with the divine breath remains unattainable, unlocatable, faceless. Anyone who perceives him starts on the road, obeys the call, goes to encounter nothing, or else something greater than anything we now have.

DIVINE WOMEN

Venice-Mestre, June 8, 1984
Interdisciplinary study organized by
the Women's Center on *Melusine*

Writing *Marine Lover, Passions élémentaires*, and *L'oubli de l'air*,* I had thought of doing a study of our relations to the elements: water, earth, fire, air. I was anxious to go back to those natural matters that constitute the origin of our bodies, of our life, of our environment, the flesh of our passions. I was obeying a deep, dark, and necessary intuition, dark even when it it is shared by other thoughts.

But, as I read *Melusine* for the first time and reread "The Little Mermaid" and other stories,[1] I discovered some of the reasons that led me to consider our relationship to sea, air, earth, fire. I understand now that this relationship has never been decoded and has therefore remained a matter of fables and monsters (particularly in the etymological meaning of the word), revealing and hiding something of our identity, of the difficulties we have in situating ourselves in relation to ourselves and to our fellows, something of the dramas and spells that captivate us, capture us, bind us, and separate us.

We still pass our daily lives in a universe that is composed and is known to be composed of four elements: air, water, fire, and earth. We are made up of these elements and we live in them. They determine, more or less freely, our attractions, our affects, our passions, our limits, our aspirations.

These elements, which, since the beginning of philosophy, have been a focus of meditation of every creation of a world, have often been misunderstood in our culture, which has tended to refuse to think about the material conditions of existence. Poetry recalls the

---

*Of these three books, only the first has been published in English: *Marine Lover of Friedrich Nietzsche*, translated by Gillian C. Gill, New York: Columbia University Press, 1990.—Tr.

1. The texts that I read or reread for this essay are, first, the story of *Melusine* as recounted by Jean (le Teinturier) d'Arras and published in 1478; the comparable stories in the Andersen and Grimm collections of fairy tales; the analyses of the Melusine myth by Jean Le Goff and Emmanuel Leroy Ladurie in *Les Annales*, May-August 1971, a special issue dedicated to "History and Structure"; *Mélusine et le chevalier au cygne* by Christian Lacouteux (Paris: Payot, 1982); *The Essence of Christianity* by Ludwig Feuerbach (translated by George Eliot, New York: Harper Torchbooks, 1957).

elements, as does science in a different way—endlessly defining new material particles that compose us and form our environment without our naming them or perceiving them, at least consciously. Our so-called human sciences and our day-to-day speech steer clear of the elements, moving forward through and with a language that forgets the matter it names and by means of which it speaks. Traces and remains of the elements are often laid down in myths and folk tales as *mysteries*, those stories of birth, initiation, love, war, death, and passion delivered in images and actions with all innocence of knowledge. Such affections have yet to be decoded, thought through, interpreted, not as a "failure" but rather as a stage in history.

Melusine is a love story in both its private and public dimensions. It corresponds to a stage in our imaginary that is still thoroughly relevant. The passions are a matter of fire and ice, of light and darkness, of water and drowning, of earth and finding or losing one's footing, and of breathing in the deepest and most secret aspects of life. Our passions are transformed or transform us into phenomena that can be watery or heavenly, solar or volcanic, blazing with light or lost in shadow, throbbing or dozing. . . . All this is conjured up for us by the cosmic cycles or the signs of the zodiac whose present mode connects with certain moments of interpretation and mutation in history—certain identity crises experienced by humanity and the world. Is it not true that in this age of sophisticated technical apparatus we still frequently turn to the Middle Ages in search of our images and secrets?

Is this because we still need a little time to dream? Or does it point to a driving need to elaborate the opacity of the subject, woman in particular, God in particular? When we question the mystery of the image and all that hides behind it, are we not in fact investigating the transmutational or transfigurational states that may be represented therein, may be figured therein without expressing the totality of a native, natal secret that is always bound up with *touch?* Fish, bird, of course! But what lies hidden behind these partial incarnations, these monstrously composite women, or indeed men, these stages in a becoming that must never be seen or unveiled either in their *physical nudity* in the wife's case, or in their *lineage* in the husband's, since the total consummation of the marriage never takes place.

These marriages—mandatory for saving the one or the other, the one and the other, in corporeal or genealogic destiny, living form or name—always remain *conditional*. No doubt, they perform a symbolic and social function. They procreate children, construct castles, cultivate the earth, build cities. All the same, love in these tales is always star-crossed. Neither flesh, nor spirit, nor body, nor name are allied, generated, regenerated, allowed to flourish. *Melusine* and the myths of the same family—particularly those of the *Chevalier au cygne* (swan knight)—enact this veiled drama of the woman's corporeal avatar and the man's symbolic avatar still separated in the consummation of their wedding.

If we look seriously at this composite and provisional incarnation of man and woman we are brought back to the sense that underlies all the other four senses, that exists or insists in them all, our first sense and the one that constitutes all our living space, all our environment: the sense of *touch*. This is the sense that travels with us from the time of our material conception to the height of our celestial grace, lightness, or glory. We have to return to touch if we are to comprehend where touch became frozen in its passage from the most elemental to the most sophisticated part of its evolution. This will mean that we need to stay both firm and mobile in our cathexes, always faithful, that is, to the dimension of touch.

We regress and we progress, way beyond all sense of sight, from the most primitive to the subtlest realm of the tactile. Everything is given to us by means of touch, a mediation that is continually forgotten. Anything that emerges into the visible realm, the images of man and the world, remains for awhile in history, but this visual birth does not fulfill all our native potentialities. The figures that have put on fleshly form have not said, not expressed all that there is to be said about the power of incarnation. In the enigmas formed by the popular or the literary imagination, in the monsters produced by culture, we may seek a sense of the darkest part of our becoming, which is the most deeply tactile.

Surely man favors the visual because it marks his exit from the life in the womb? His victory over the maternal power and his opportunity to overcome a mother whom he experiences as amorphous, formless, a pit, a chasm in which he risks losing his form?

Melusine is clearly a story about the relationship to the mother, and mother nature, and how she fits into society. This myth, like "The Little Mermaid," presents us with the passage from *life in the womb* to *life in the air:* a life situated in ambiguous relations to a society of couples who give birth to offspring but have difficulty with *love*. Because we are still half-fish, half-birds? Not yet women, born women (or men, in fact)? Not yet human and divine? Two that go in parallel. This also means that there are no couples, or very few, who are fertile in any but the strictly bodily sense. Which explains the fact that mothers and fathers are always facing a dilemma, are forever paralyzed by duties that are not the core of our destiny, which is to generate the human, the divine, within us and among us.

How are we to understand the stages taken, the delays suffered in our progress to become divine women—half creatures of sea, half creatures of air—stages that in fact are followed by the representations of the trinitary God (father, son-fish, spirit-bird)?[2]

When we take a close look at the myth of Melusine, its range of diffusion, its different versions, we are in fact investigating something that attracts us, fascinates us even, like a mystery, a key to our identity.

I am far from suggesting that today we must once again deify ourselves as did our ancestors with their animal totems, that we have to regress to siren goddesses, who fight against men gods. Rather I think we must not merely instigate a return to the *cosmic*, but also ask ourselves why we have been held back from becoming *divine women*.

It is important for us to remember that we have to respect nature in its cycles, its life, its growth; it is important for us to recall that events in history, that History itself, *cannot and must not conceal cosmic events and rhythms*. But all this must be done in the context of entering further into womanhood, not moving backwards. If we resist hierarchies (the man/woman hierarchy, or state/woman, or a certain form of God/woman, or machine/woman), only to fall back into *the power* (*pouvoir*) of nature/woman, animal/woman, even matriarchs/women, women/women, we have not made much progress. Even as we respect the universe as one of our most vital and cultural dimensions, as one of the macrocosmic keys to our microcosm, we must thereby enter further into womanhood, and not become more alien to ourselves than we were, more in exile than we were.

---

2. The constellation we call Pisces is composed of two fishes: one goes upwards to the heavens, the other goes down to the earth, the sea. From the reading of these myths that concern us here, it would seem that the fish going upward is exclusively a male, the fish going down, a female. The descent into the sea is interpreted as "fabled" and later "diabolical," whereas in fact it also connotes a return to, and a fidelity toward, the original fertility. Moreover, these fairy tales often present woman as bird, usually in a derogatory fashion. Yet we should not forget that in certain cultures of the far East, such as India or Tibet, the dragon (half serpent-fish, half bird?) is the emblem of life and the divine word, of the creative and saving word of life on earth. This is only one example of the way contemporary Western writers have diabolically transformed and interpreted an ancient symbol of the potency (*puissance*) of life and word.

☆

Man is able to exist because God helps him to define his gender (*genre*), helps him orient his finiteness by reference to infinity. The revival of religious feeling can in fact be interpreted as the rampart man raises in defense of his very maleness.

To posit a gender, a God is necessary: *guaranteeing the infinite*.[3] Science does not have the capacity to be constantly positing the infinite of the finite. In fact it is little concerned with positing the finite of the infinite. Science makes limits by closing things off. Thereby banning becoming? Willfully? Or does science have no will? A science that has no subject assumes a theory or a vision of the world that has *no will*.

Are we able to go on living if we have no will? This seems impossible. We have to will. It is necessary, not for our morality, but for our life. It is the condition of our becoming. In order to will, we have to have a goal. The goal that is most valuable is to go on *becoming*, infinitely.

In order to become, it is essential to have a gender or an essence (consequently a sexuate essence) as *horizon*. Otherwise, becoming remains partial and subject to the subject. When we become parts or multiples without a future of our own this means simply that we are leaving it up to the other, or the Other of the other, to put us together.

To become means fulfilling the wholeness of what we are capable of being. Obviously, this road never ends. Are we more perfect than in the past? This is not certain. Could this be because woman has no gender through which she can become? And man, clearly, is able to complete his essence only if he claims to be separate as a *gender*. If he has no existence in his gender, he lacks his relation to the infinite and, in fact, to finiteness.

To avoid that finiteness, man has sought out a unique *male* God. God has been created out of man's gender. He scarcely sets limits within Himself and between Himself: He is father, son, spirit. Man has not allowed himself to be defined by another gender: the female. His unique God is assumed to correspond to the human race (*genre*

---

3. This interpretation of the "essence of man" and of the difference between man and animal is developed by Feuerbach in *The Essence of Christianity*, especially in the introduction. Readers interested in an exact understanding of "Divine Women" should refer to this essay.

humain), which we know is not neuter or neutral from the point of view of the difference of the sexes.

It is true that Christianity tells us that God is in three persons, three manifestations, and that the third stage of the manifestation occurs as *a wedding between the spirit and the bride.* Is this supposed to inaugurate the divine for, in, with women? The female?

Divinity is what we need to become free, autonomous, sovereign. No human subjectivity, no human society has ever been established without the help of the divine. There comes a time for destruction. But, before destruction is possible, God or the gods must exist.

If women have no God, they are unable either to communicate or commune with one another. They need, we need, an infinite if they are to share *a little.* Otherwise sharing implies fusion-confusion, division, and dislocation within themselves, among themselves. If I am unable to form a relationship with some horizon of accomplishment for my gender, I am unable to share while protecting my becoming.

Our theological tradition presents some difficulty as far as God in the feminine gender is concerned. There is no *woman* God, no female trinity: mother, daughter, spirit. This paralyzes the infinite of becoming a woman since she is fixed in the role of mother through whom the *son* of God is made flesh. The most influential representation of God in our culture over the last two thousand years has been a male trinitary God and a virgin mother: a mother of the son of God whose alliance with the father is given little consideration. Is she the wife? By what mediation? The spirit? Who is represented as an angel, a young man, or a bird? The virgin's relations with the Father always remain in the shadow. Just as the Father himself? Her relations with the spirit are presented a number of times: the annunciation and the Pentecost, at the very least. The angel (plus bird in the habitual iconography) and the fire would seemingly be the representatives or vehicles of the spirit.

Is the angel of the Annunciation an appearance of the Father (as well as of the spirit)? Coming to visit and announce the virgin's fertile condition. But the Father is not single. He is three. The virgin is alone of her sex. Without a daughter or love between them, without a way of becoming divine except through her son: God-man, without a divine bridegroom. Unless we have known only two stages in Western culture and the third, the stage of the spirit and the wedding with the bride, has yet to come.

Would this correspond to what the astrologers announce as the stage of science? Which stage? And this era is prefigured or prophesied in the Old and the New Testament.

If this were the case, women would have some reason to be interested in religion, in science, in the relations between them, since women are represented as receivers of the spirit and not just as rather malformed monsters: manifestations of the eras of transition, between this incarnation and some other.

☆

The love of God has often been a haven for women. They are the guardians of the religious tradition. Certain women mystics have been among those rare women to achieve real social influence, notably in politics.

Religion marks the place of the absolute *for us*, its path, the hope of its fulfillment. All too often that fulfillment has been postponed or transferred to some transcendental time and place. It has not been interpreted as the infinite that resides within us and among us, the god in us, the Other for us, becoming with and in us—as yet manifest only through his creation (the Father), present in his form (the son), mediator between the two (spirit). Here the capital letter designates the horizon of fulfillment of a gender, not a transcendent entity that exists outside becoming.

This God, are we capable of imagining it as a woman? Can we dimly see it as the perfection of our subjectivity? Which assumes respect for these two dimensions: the nocturnal-internal dimension of motherhood, whose threshold is closed during gestation and opened (too wide?) for and after birthing; the dimension between darkness and light occupied by the female, whose threshold is always half open, in-finite. The becoming of women is never over and done with, is always in gestation. A woman's subjectivity must accommodate the dimensions of mother and lover as well as the union between the two.

Our tradition presents and represents the radiant glory of the mother, but rarely shows us a fulfilled woman. And it forces us to make murderous choices: either mother (given that a *boy* child is what makes us truly mothers) or woman (prostitute and property of the male). We have no female trinity. But, as long as woman lacks a divine made in her image she cannot establish her subjectivity or achieve a goal of her own. She lacks an ideal that would be her goal

63

or path in becoming. Woman scatters and becomes an agent of destruction and annihilation because she has no other of her own that she can become.

The (male) ideal other has been imposed upon women by men. Man is supposedly woman's more perfect other, her model, her essence. The most human and the most divine goal woman can conceive is to become *man*. If she is to become woman, if she is to accomplish her female subjectivity, woman needs a god who is a figure for the perfection of *her* subjectivity.

The impotence, the formlessness, the deformity associated with women, the way they are equated with something other than the human and split between the human and the inhuman (half-woman, half-animal), their duty to be adorned, masked, and made up, etc., rather than being allowed *their own* physical, bodily beauty, their own skin, their own form(s), all this is symptomatic of the fact that women lack a female god who can open up the perspective in which *their* flesh can be transfigured.

The only diabolical thing about women is their lack of a God and the fact that, deprived of God, they are forced to comply with models that do not match them, that exile, double, mask them, cut them off from themselves and from one another, stripping away their ability to move forward into love, art, thought, toward their ideal and divine fulfillment.

Women have rarely used their beauty as a weapon *for themselves,* even more rarely as a *spiritual* weapon. The body's splendor has rarely been used as a lever to advance self-love, self-fulfillment.

Maternal beauty has been glorified in our religious and social traditions, but womanly beauty for centuries has been seen merely as a trap for the other. The transfiguration of a female body by beauty, the active share that the woman can have in that transfiguration, are today often misunderstood. Perhaps they have been forgotten. Beauty is not presented or represented as the spiritual predicate of the flesh. Yet, it is not impossible to imagine that a body can be, can above all become, intelligent or stupid, that our relation to corporal love can be actively aesthetic or passively abject, reduced: for example, to a pseudoanimality (animals themselves are beautiful in their sexual displays; bestial is an animal quality negatively attributed to man) or to motherhood, with its associations to bodily deformity and the link often made between it and chastity.

Female beauty is always considered a *garment* ultimately designed to attract the other into the self. It is almost never perceived as a manifestation of, an appearance by a phenomenon expressive of interiority—whether of love, of thought, of flesh. We look at ourselves in the mirror to *please someone*, rarely to interrogate the state of our body or our spirit, rarely for ourselves and in search of our own becoming. The mirror almost always serves to reduce us to a pure exteriority—of a very particular kind. It functions as a possible way to constitute screens between the other and myself. In a way quite different from the mucous membranes or the skin that serve as living, porous, fluid media to achieve communion as well as difference, the mirror is a frozen—and polemical—weapon to keep us apart. I give only my double up to love. I do not yield myself up as body, flesh, as immediate—and geological, genealogical—affects. The mirror signifies the constitution of a fabricated (female) other that I shall put forward as an instrument of seduction in my place. I seek to be seductive and to be content with images of which I theoretically remain the artisan, the artist. I have yet to unveil, unmask, or veil myself *for me*—to veil myself so as to achieve self-contemplation, for example, to let my gaze travel over myself so as to limit my exposure to the other and repossess my own gestures and garments, thus nestling back into my vision and contemplation of myself. Which is not a kind of cold narcissism but rather a way that, as an adult, I can supplement and support the different houses, the different bodies that have borne me, wrapped me, rocked me, embraced me, enlaced me. The mirror, and indeed the gaze, are frequently used as weapons or tools that ward off touching and hold back fluidity, even the liquid embrace of the gaze.

Though necessary at times as a separating tool, the mirror—and the gaze when it acts as a mirror—ought to remain a means and not an end that enforces my obedience. The mirror should support, not undermine my incarnation. All too often it sends back superficial, flat images. There are other images that generate volume better than the reflection in the glass. To work at beauty is at least as much a matter of working at gestures as they relate to space and to other people as it is a matter of gazing, usually in anxiety, at one's mirror. The mirror freezes our becoming breath, our becoming space. Our becoming bird, perhaps? Though it may at times help us to emerge, to move out of the water, the mirror blocks our energies, freezes us in our tracks, clips our wings. What protects me from the other and allows me to move toward him or her is more often the settling of a space, an enclave of air rather than the interposition of mirrors and glasses whose cutting edge all too often threatens to turn against me. Once we have left the *waters* of the womb, we have to construct a space for ourselves in the *air* for the rest of our time on earth—air in which we can breathe and sing freely, in which we can perform and move at will. Once we were fishes. It seems that we are destined to become birds. None of this is possible unless the air opens up freely to our movements.

To construct and inhabit our airy space is essential. It is the space of bodily autonomy, of free breath, free speech and song, of performing on the stage of life. We still are not *born women*. We are still and always guardians of the phylogenesis of the human race (with man, on the other hand, guarding its ontogenesis?), we are still and always between different incarnations, and devoted to the task of assisting man in his incarnation: a terrestrial and marine place for man's conception and gestation, with the mother feeding him, guiding his steps, fostering his growth, aiding him to develop in relation to his established gender, his Man-God. Thus women are traditionally the guardians of the multiform embryo, of the growing child, of the suffering man. This is apparently the role women must fill in the redemption of the world. And, it seems that women go to heaven only once the son has ascended in glory and comes back to lead his mother on high.

This vocation for collaborating in the redemption of the world through suffering and chastity (which is viewed as privation) ought not to remain our only destiny, our only horizon, should not constitute the only means or path to our fulfillment as women.[4*]

Suffering does not in any way constitute a perfection, it is merely a means of restoration. As such, suffering corresponds not to a kind of saintliness but rather to an established kind of human perversity. Suffering, if it lasts more than a redemptive moment, is simply a

4. *S'épanouir* corresponds to one of the three translations for the etymology of the word *to be* that Martin Heidegger gives: "to live, to emerge, to linger or endure." It means to accomplish one's form. (*An Introduction to Metaphysics*, translated by Ralph Manheim, New Haven and London: Yale University Press, 1959, p. 72).

*For the verb *s'épanouir*, which is rendered as "emerge" in Manheim's translation from the German, I have preferred the verb *fulfill*.—Tr.

denial of the divine. "If feeling seems to thee a glorious attribute, it is then, *per se*, a divine attribute to thee" (Feuerbach, p. 63).

"God is the mirror of man" (Feuerbach, p. 63). Woman has no mirror wherewith to become woman. Having a God and becoming one's gender go hand in hand. God is the other that we absolutely cannot be without. In order to *become*, we need some shadowy perception of achievement; not a fixed objective, not a One postulated to be immutable but rather a cohesion and a horizon that assures us the passage between past and future, the bridge of a present *that remembers*, that is not sheer oblivion and loss, not a crumbling away of existence, a failure, simply, to take note.

A *female* god is still to come. We are not purely redeeming spirits, not pure flesh, not a veil for the wisdom of the world, not mere mothers, not mere devils. . . . All these predicates speak to something of us, often of us as we are seen by men and as men need us to be.

How is our God to be imagined? Or is it our god? Do we possess a quality that can reverse the predicate to the subject, as Feuerbach does for *God* and *man* in the analysis of *The Essence of Christianity*? If there is no one quality, which of the many would we choose to conceive our becoming perfect women? This is not a luxury but a *necessity*, the need for a finalized, theoretical, and practical activity that would be both speculative and moral. Every man (according to Feuerbach) and every woman who is not fated to remain a slave to the logic of the essence of man, must imagine a God, an objective-subjective place or path whereby the self could be coalesced in space and time: unity of instinct, heart, and knowledge, unity of nature and spirit, condition for the abode and for saintliness. God alone can save us, keep us safe. The feeling or experience of a positive, objective, glorious existence, the feeling of subjectivity, is essential for us. Just like a God who helps us and leads us in the path of becoming, who keeps track of our limits and our infinite possibilities—as women—who inspires our projects. These might include not just *opposition to, criticism of* but also *positing new values* that would essentially be divine. To have a goal is essentially a religious move (according to Feuerbach's analysis). Only the religious, within and without us, is fundamental enough to allow us to discover, affirm, achieve certain *ends* (without being locked up in the prison of effect—or effects). Our goal has always come to us women from outside: from man, child, city. We have failed to place our goal *inside as well as outside ourselves*, failed to love, failed to *will* ourselves and one another. Because this can only be a divine project. God conceives and loves himself. That part of God has always been denied us. Thus we women have become weak, formless, insecure, aggressive, devoted to the other because unaware of ourselves, submissive to the other because we were unable to establish our own order. If we are not to obey the other, we have to set a goal of our own, make our own law or laws. If we are to escape slavery it is not enough to destroy the master. Only the divine offers us freedom—enjoins it upon us. Only a God constitutes a rallying point for us that can let us free—nothing else. These words are but a statement of *reason*. So far it requires no faith other than the faith in the possibility of our autonomy, our salvation, of a love that would not just redeem but glorify us in full self-awareness: thought directed at the self and for the self that is free to love but not obliged.

To be capable of autonomy, to be capable of our God (still in the darkness, already made flesh, mediation between), is this not the test women must undergo if we are to become what we are and realize in a different mode our individual and collective task? Community means only dependence as long as each man, each woman, is not free and sovereign. Love of other without love of self, without love of God, implies the submission of the female one, the other, and of the whole of the social body.

No one has truly taught us love of God. Only love of neighbor. But how can one love one's neighbor without loving God? This is no more than a moralism of guilt, impossible to sustain, a kind of egotism or even death. Certain social doctrines, certain political regimes have already shown us how difficult it is to "love one's neighbor" without loving God. The obstacle is also an economic one. Men seem to lack the generosity to care for the good of others before caring for their own. God is man's good and his goods. Love of neighbor is an ethical consequence of becoming divine. To claim that man is capable of caring about his neighbor's good, careless of his own, seems an idealist and utopic hypothesis that brings in its wake physical and psychic misery, the decline of the mother-earth culture, and of the values of speech and spiritual autonomy.

Love of God has nothing moral in and of itself. It merely shows the way. It is the incentive for a more perfect becoming. It marks the horizon between the more past and the more future, the more passive and the more active—permanent and always in tension. God forces us to do nothing except *become*. The only task, the only obligation laid upon us is: to become divine men and women, to become perfectly, to refuse to allow parts of ourselves to shrivel and die that have the potential for growth and fulfillment.

And in this we still resemble plants. We climb toward God and remain in Him, without killing the mother earth where our roots lie, without denying the sky either. Rooted in the earth, fed by rain and spring waters, we grow and flourish in the air, thanks to the light from the sky, the warmth of the sun.

There is no *individual law* that concerns divine becoming, no *collective law* passed down to the race of woman. . . . But, if we do not have that—divine—perspective, we—as divine—cannot incarnate our gender or make a race.

Can the word *woman* be subject? predicate? If it can be neither one nor the other, what status does the word have in discourse? The status of "women" as indeterminate plural, as obscure part of the human race. Must we assume that man is "women" (one + one + one . . .) *plus* a penis? or that God is "women" (all women), *plus* something that fences in the infinite: a difficult figuration of a relation men have to their penis or their gender? Since only man and God are subjects.

This "women" would amount to a kind of chaotic, amorphous, archaic multiple which, if it is ever to achieve a form, needs some representation of unity to be imposed upon it. "Women" would be like the soup, the clay, the earth and blood, the water, the ocean, out of which man emerges as man, and God as God. Woman, the one, single, *unique*, would at best be viewed as a place of procreation or of partition into objects of seduction.

If there is ever to be a consciousness of self in the female camp, each woman will have to situate herself freely in relation to herself, not just in relation to the community, the couple, the family. Feuerbach writes that without the woman-mother (but he seems to take little account of the difference between woman and mother, hence there is no correspondence with a possible state of identity for the woman as woman) there is no God. The mother of God is the keystone of theology, of the Father-son-spirit relationship. Without the mother of God, there can be no God. And Feuerbach adds that Protestants, who have done away with the mother of God—she who gives birth to the Lord as flesh—should logically have renounced God purely and simply: "Where faith in the Mother of God sinks, there also sinks faith in the Son of God, and in God as the Father. The Father is a truth only where the Mother is a truth. Love is in and by itself essentially feminine in its nature. The belief in the love of God is the belief in the feminine principle as divine. Love apart from living nature is an anomaly, a phantom. Behold in love the holy necessity and depth of Nature" (*The Essence of Christianity,* p. 72).

Feuerbach claims that we are sick today because God is sick. God undergoes his own process of development: He "has wrestled himself out of the obscurity of confused feelings and impulses into the clearness of knowledge," the "nervous tremours of darkness precede the joyful consciousness of light" (p. 89).

In our tradition hasn't God always been sick because he never married? Except in the forms of annunciation our God never speaks to us of the joy, the splendor, the fulfillment that lies in the alliance of the sexes. He remains bound to a father or a mother, and a fault—which?—that must be redeemed if love is to become, or again become, possible.

We have often been told that weddings take place only in heaven. But, from the representation we have of heaven can we deduce something of a female divinity? Establish some *concrete* qualities of divine life that have often been forgotten in the transcendence of the all-powerful God? Of God the Father we know very little. Making images of Him is no simple matter and remains subject to rigid rules. But we can ask ourselves whether the promises of heaven made to us do not imply something of the female gender that has been excluded from God. In heaven, there will be music, colors, movement, dancing . . . none of the austerity often attributed to God the Father. Doesn't heaven constitute an actualization of qualities that have been left to women but in women become instruments of unheavenly seduction? The predicates of heaven are often sensual, artistic. Religion is in fact a major producer of art. And Freud would have it that art corresponds to the sublimation of hysteria, that female neurosis par excellence.

But it seems that women have no God to sublimate their hysteria—they can merely give birth to the redeeming God. Why would women have no God to allow them to fulfill their *gender*? So that heaven does not come to pass on earth? So that women should remain the ones who give birth to the child god, the suffering god, the redeemer son? Is this a way for women to become divine in their gender? And man? Neither men nor women are able to grow to adulthood together, to become gods together. Woman's not becoming God is a loss for herself and for the community. Perhaps for God. Certainly for the fulfillment of the universe, which she brings into being through her *female* sex according to certain traditions. If she is to be faithful to her natural and political gender, if she is to make that gender divine, women must accept it and fulfill it as a limit that is also *morphological.*

This divinity of woman is still hidden, veiled. Could it be what "man" seeks even as he rapes it?

We women, sexed according to our gender, lack a God to share, a word to share and to become. Defined as the often dark, even occult mother-substance of the word of men, we are in need of our *subject,* our *substantive,* our *word,* our *predicates:* our elementary sentence, our basic rhythm, our morphological identity, our generic incarnation, our genealogy.

To be the term of the other is nothing enviable. It paralyzes us in our becoming. As divinity or goddess of and for man, we are deprived of our own ends and means. It is essential that we be God *for ourselves* so that we can be divine for the other, not idols, fetishes, symbols that have already been outlined or determined (see *The Essence of Christianity,* p. 182). It is equally essential that we should be daughter-gods in the relationship with our mothers, and that we cease to hate our mothers in order to enter into submissiveness to the father-husband. We cannot love if we have no memory of a native passiveness in relation to our mothers, of our primitive attachment to her, and hers to us.

Current theory, even theological theory, makes women out to be monsters of hatred and thus makes us submit to an existing order. Does respect for God made flesh not imply that we should incarnate God within us and in our sex: daughter-woman-mother? Yet this duty is never imposed upon us—quite the contrary. What a strange error in human ethics! By our culture, our religion.

This error is protracted and encouraged by the spiritual technicians: the psychologists, psychoanalysts, etc. And yet, without the possibility that God might be made flesh as a woman, through the mother and the daughter, and in their relationships, no real constructive help can be offered to a woman. If the divine is absent in woman, and among women, there can be no possibility of changing, converting her primary affects.

The God we know, the gods we have known for centuries, are men; they show and hide the different aspects of man. He (they)

71

do(es) not represent the qualities or predicates of the *female* made God. Which explains, perhaps, why *women who have grown used to the God/s of men will have no more to do with Him/them* (as men do?) and are ready to give up their own divinity. They renounce the path of becoming or being women. For how can that goal, that project, be sustained without a divine that marks or establishes its realization, that figures its incarnation, its mediations?

When women get bogged down in their search for freedom, for liberation, there seem to be many themes: the absence of a God of their own and inadequate management of the symbolic. The two things are linked and necessary to the constitution of an identity and a community. Many women have made or are making great efforts to fall back under the thrall of the phallocratic and patriarchal monopoly on values. They lack, we still lack, the affirmation and definition of values *of our own*, values often condemned by women themselves, even in dealings with other women. This leaves us in our infancy, in our bondage, slaves to male paradigms and to the archaic powers and fears of elementary struggles for life that are divided between submission to a technical imperialism alien to us and regression to *magical* thinking.

According to this world, these worlds, female identity always comes down to empirical parameters that prevent a woman, and the world of women, from getting them*selves* together as a unit. The sexual-familial dimension remains one of these parameters. "Are you a virgin?" "Are you married?" "Who is your husband?" "Do you have any children?" these are the questions always asked, which allow us to place a woman. She is constituted from outside in relation to a social *function*, instead of to a female identity and autonomy. Fenced in by these functions, how can a woman maintain a margin of singleness for herself, a nondeterminism that would allow her to become and remain herself? This margin of freedom and potency (*puissance*) that gives us the authority yet to grow, to affirm and fulfill ourselves as individuals and members of a community, can be ours only if a God in the feminine gender can define it and keep it for us. As an other that we have yet to make actual, as a region of life, strength, imagination, creation, which exists for us both within and beyond, as our possibility of a present and a future.

Is not God the name and the place that holds the promise of a new chapter in history and that also denies this can happen? Still invisible? Still to be discovered? To be incarnated? Archi-ancient and forever future.

72

WOMEN, THE SACRED, MONEY

Aix-en-Provence, November 17, 1984
C.E.F.U.P. Conference at the University of Aix-Marseille
on "Woman and Money"

The following five questions summarize the issues I see raised in regard to the function of women in *sacrificial* societies such as our own:

1. What meaning does sacrifice have in relation to cosmic temporality and rhythms?
2. What rites and what systems of exchange can be set up among women? Today? In the future?
3. Is charity work performed by women complicit in the sacrifice?
4. If the reproductive and nourishing function of mothers goes unpaid, does this not mean that the child becomes an object of exchange among women?
5. Are our societies inevitably unbalanced because the natural and cultural infrastructure—women, mothers, theoreticians, both male and female—are paid either nothing or very little?

☆

1. It seems we are unable to eliminate or suppress the phenomenon of religion. It reemerges in different forms, some of them perverse: sectarianism, theoretical or political dogmatism, religiosity. . . . Therefore, it is crucial that we rethink religion, and especially religious structures, categories, initiations, rules, and utopias, all of which have been masculine for centuries. Keeping in mind that today these religious structures often appear under the name of science and technology.

Most of our societies have been built on sacrifice. Social space exists only through an immolation. René Girard (as well as Mircea Eliade, for example) offers numerous instances of this.[1] Girard's

1. Notably in *Violence and the Sacred*, translated by Patrick Gregory, Baltimore: Johns Hopkins University Press, 1977, and in *Things Hidden Since the Foundation of the World*,

demonstration can be applied to a large number of social phenomena. But he says little about how his work is relevant to women. Except perhaps in the chapter of *Violence and the Sacred* that is devoted to the women companions of Dionysus? That example is too obvious and largely irrelevant, in my view. It would seem to me to be more appropriate to inquire whether, under the sacrificed victim, another victim is often hidden. If we are not to sink once again into persecutions of man by men, or of men by God, it is equally critical to investigate the location, as well as the subjective and objective setup found at the origin of the substitution.

At what point in time are nature, men, and gods consecrated by certain ritual acts and words? At what point does cosmic time get divided up into the periodicity of ritual? How does it come about that men cease to regulate their meetings, their communities, their prayers exclusively in accordance with natural cycles: morning, noon, and night; the different seasons; the solar and lunar periods; the various positions of the earth, or the other planets, etc.? Some part of that natural order has prevailed in certain time periods and is being sought in our own, notably by those who are going back to astrology, sometimes to ritual, though with no attempt to abolish or revise the sacrificial setup. Every new discovery is or becomes aimed at a sacrifice. Only rarely does some initiative serve to inaugurate a new rhythm, a new mode of social living, a covenant that needs no scapegoat.

Is it impossible for a community to gather together morning, noon, or night without needing a sacrifice? The meeting could ritually celebrate our joy in seeing one another and exchanging greetings. Why could a collective group not be formed on the basis of social and cosmic goals without feeling a need to sacrifice, or eat the sacrificial object, etc.? Would speech not finally find its place therein, instead of allowing the other rites to take over? Speech could potentially be the opposite of rite, rather than its substitute. All too often rite seems to take the place of speech.

Why has speech failed? What has it lacked? Why do we kill, break, and eat as a sign of covenant? So as to do away with some act of violence? Which? Resulting from what? And is there no way to

---

translated by Stephen Bann and Michael Metteer, Stanford: Stanford University Press, 1987. Girard shows how each social era is reconstructed on the basis of a sacrifice, of some cathartic immolation that is essential to the return to relational order. This type of explanation, of functioning, seems to me to correspond to the masculine model of sexuality described by Freud: tension, discharge, return to homeostasis, etc.

analyze what made speech so inappropriate that this sacrificial act became necessary? Could it be, for example, because there is no harmony between words, actions, bodies? Certain cultures manage—or used to manage—to marry actions, words, macro- and microcosmic natures, and gods: are these cultures sacrificial? If so, how do they organize sexual difference and the systems of exchange?

Thus, in certain Eastern countries, ritual and individual prayer consists in bodily exercise that is either personal or collective: yoga, tai chi, karate, song, dance, the tea ceremony, flower arranging. There is no sacrifice of the other, and yet there is a much richer spirituality as well as a more fertile eroticism. Even though modern life has had some impact on these fundamentally religious practices, they nonetheless show greater respect for sexual difference in their concern with body positions, in the images of their gods (who are often shown coupling), in their calendars, horaries, etc. The organs of the body are considered and situated according to their masculine or feminine energy circuits, according to the seasons, the hour of the day, etc. The sacred consists in honoring nature, not immolating it. Its discipline includes all the dimensions of life and stresses a culture of health as both spiritual and divine. The community's duty is to organize a space-time that is attuned to both micro- and macrocosmic needs.

Thus one achieves ethical, social, and religious being by attending to the season, the time of day, the passing moment, and honoring the living order, rather than destroying it, although destruction itself is part of the great natural cycles and tends to signal growth and a new beginning.

Is this a utopia? Can a society live without sacrifices, without aggression? Perhaps, if it obeys the moment of cosmic temporality. The sacrificial order overlays the natural rhythms with a different and *cumulative* temporality that dispenses and prevents us from attending to the moment. Once this occurs imprecisions multiply and grow. A *catharsis* becomes necessary.

Could attention to the moment be enough of a catharsis? Physiological, cosmic, social metabolisms can work together. To achieve this harmony, there is no need for sacrifice to regulate the collective order. Once again: is this a utopia? Surely, it is rather the sacrificial societies who live or survive on persistent deception? Which leads us to reduce certain religious traditions to the sacrificial element. Christ is usually represented on the cross in places of worship. Festivals, miracles, mystery, play little part in our churches. Yet the

technocratic society that has been set up and managed by men alone. This is still true today, perhaps more than ever.

How, within this society, can women initiate certain rites that allow them to live and become women in all dimensions? How are systems of exchange to be set up *among women?* I know of no society that has lived from market exchanges *among women.* Perhaps such a one existed very long ago? Perhaps such a one exists very far away? But where are the traces of a *currency* among women? And of a God *among* women? We know about certain rites for or among women: rites of healing, all too often called witchcraft (even when it was prophetic of certain trends in modern medicine that signal a return to old traditions), sabbatical rites that are close to the cosmic. These rites are often linked to the moon at certain times and in certain places. And women today are still claiming that part of their heritage, despite those divine goddesses of fertility: Gaia, Demeter. . . . Most of the gods of the *universe* start out as goddesses. The solar goddesses are obliterated or displaced when the universe is taken over by the men-gods, especially by Zeus and his son Apollo. This domination of the cosmic world by the gods by means of the couple of a unique God-Father and an all-powerful son, erases the fact that mothers and daughters once presided as goddesses over the solar seasons and, together, protected the fertility of the earth in its flowers and fruits. Furthermore, the solar rule of men sets a pejorative connotation on the moon, which is also a source of life and fertility. When astrological power in its godly aspect is taken away from women, earth suffers the threat of sterility.

A fertile earth and a valuable commodity are not the same thing. Not infrequently these two productions are opposed economically, and the second is preferred to the first. But when the goddesses of cosmic fertility were suppressed to found so-called rich societies, certain problems arose. Every time man or men seek to build an economic order at the expense of the earth, that order becomes sterile, repressive, and destructive.

Could it be that the sacrifice of natural fertility is the original sacrifice? It leads to an economic superstructure (falsely labeled infrastructure) that has no respect for the infrastructure of natural fertility. In accordance with this system, many economic aberrations occur: certain areas of land are not cultivated, a proportion of products are thrown away, one part of the population goes hungry, even in industrialized countries. What currency is involved here? Because this is definitely a question of *a failure of equivalence between a standard currency and a use value:* those products of the earth that are necessary for food, clothing, and lodging. Today there are occasions when the products and the productive capacity of the earth are annihilated in order to inflate an unsecured currency.

Whether consciously or not, sacrificial societies perpetuate the unconsidered destruction of the products of the earth and their possible reproduction. And yet ultimately these and not advanced weaponry and sophisticated techniques are the only *guarantees* of exchange value. What, in fact, is the point of setting up powerful nations when their populations are dying of hunger and have no more habitable space? Under the sacrifice of animal or human is hidden the sacrifice of the plant and the disappearance of the goddesses of natural fertility.

Yet it is not a matter of simply returning to the goddesses of the earth, even if this were in our power. We need to keep hold of them and establish (or reestablish) a social system that reflects their values, their fertility. It is idle to revive old myths if we are unable to celebrate them and use them to constitute a social system, a temporal system. Is this in our power?

Let us imagine that it is possible: will Gaia or Demeter be enough? What shall we do with Kore? Persephone? Diana? And with Aphrodite? Are we not always at least two? How are those two to be allied within us? among us? How can we affirm together those elementary values, those natural kinds of fruitfulness, celebrate them, keep them, preserve them, make currency of them while becoming or remaining women?

According to Feuerbach, no affirmation of gender or humanity is possible without a God, probably a trinity. Women, traditionally cast as mothers of the gods, have no God or gods of their own to fulfill their gender, whether as individuals or as a community (See "Divine Women"in this volume).

☆

3. When we ask a woman to work for nothing, when we, as women, refuse to accept or seek society's remuneration for our work, that constitutes a *repression,* or a *willingness to acquiesce to censorship of a desire to trade.* Little girls play shop with great pleasure, spontaneously, untaught, much more often than boys do. Where do they learn this game, which goes in step with their rapid acquisition of language and their talkativeness? These symbolic exchanges occur

much earlier in girls than in boys. How and why are they then repressed and censored? For the benefit of what male social system? At the cost of what *sacrifice* (or sacrifices)? As long as women never become conscious of this repression, as long as they ignore and deny it, they will perpetuate it. It is thought to be normal, moral, a sign of good policy, for a woman to receive no payment, or low payment, to be asked to do *charity work*. Especially if the woman does intellectual work? Especially if she works for women's liberation? I am using this expression in the widest possible sense. When, for example, a woman shares her knowledge and experience with a larger female public, this is a contribution to women's liberation. Unless of course the experience in question prevents the woman and her peers from positioning themselves as women in society and culture, discourages them from seeking their own identity, deprives them of the hope for a future different from the past, different from their lives as mothers and/or men.

It seems impossible to make any durable and deep impact on social relations, language, art in general, without modifying the economic system of exchanges. The one goes with the other. Sometimes one kind of modification leads the way, sometimes the other, but both are indispensable to social change. We cannot decide, or try, to free ourselves from one order without changing its modes of operation. The one demands the other. A change in economic style does not necessarily entail any real change in *relations among women*. On the other hand, a restructuring of social relations among women necessitates the establishment of an economy that is suited to them, implies a respect for an economy among women.

For lack of an order of exchange, women must obey the law of consumption without rites or sacraments. The totemic meal permits the partial exorcism of the murder of the victim. Lacking rites or words to designate it as such, this consumption becomes ever more dangerous and generates various kinds of pathology. In this way all that has been blindly sacrificed turns violent and engenders persecution among male and female consumers. Freud describes the murder of the father for us, the origins of the primeval horde when the ancestor is devoured, and the threat of war between the "brothers" before and after this ritual crime. Is the risk not greater if there is no rite? And no modification in the style of the society?

Perhaps it is not essential for every society to found itself upon a sacrifice. But, for this to occur, social functioning has to be ensured in some other way. The relation to space-time must be modified and micro- and macrocosmic rhythms must be trusted. This will entail a reduction—without new sacrifice—in *the condensation of time, the concentration of space,* which have been built upon immolation—of man, of animals, more secretly of plants and growing things, of our elementary food and space, etc.

4. It is clear that our societies assume that *the mother should feed her child for free,* before and after the birth, and that she should remain the nurse of man and of society. She is *the totem before any totem is designated,* identified, represented. This state of affairs must be understood if we are to learn how a woman, or women, can find a place without remaining shadowy nurses. This traditional role that is allotted to women almost ritually paralyzes male society as well and permits the continued destruction of the natural reserves of life. It sustains the illusion that food should come to us free, and, in any case, can never fail us. In the same way, women could never fail us, especially mothers. A certain number of works of fiction describe a world where there is a radical separation of the sexes. Yet none, to my knowledge, envisions a world without mothers. Obviously there are real life and fictitious stories about "test-tube babies," for example.[4] But this is still a case of playing with the maternal function. An artificial matrix is still not an artificial nurse, at least postnatally. How old must these children of art be before mothers are made obsolete? How much will they cost? What changes will be brought about as a result of mass-producing these laboratory offspring: economic changes, affective changes, cultural changes, etc.?

Calculating how much a child costs is enough to shock anyone, or almost. Yet one doesn't have to be a specialist in human psychology to ponder the question.

---

4. As I reread this text that I wrote two years ago I am struck by how rapidly things can change on the technical level while ethical evolution insofar as the subjective identity of women is concerned proceeds much more slowly. You need only listen to the testimony of women who have been adoptive, surrogate, or artificially inseminated mothers, to be convinced of this. There is always the same pathos, the same generosity, with no guarantor of any really responsible subjectivity. Women allow themselves to be manipulated by technocrats just as they did by patriarchs in times gone by. If proof of this were needed, it can be found in the increasing erosion of women's reproductive freedom and the failure of science to advance research into contraception. The point is always to reduce women to their role as mothers with no thought of their freedom or, indeed, of the future of their children.

Freud never imagined such things would be possible (at least as far as I am aware) and he tells us that *money is anal* and, moreover, that *children believe they are born from the anus.* He does not make the connection between the child and the currency of exchange, or at least I do not recall finding this in any of his work. But it is worth investigating how our social system forces *little girls who love to play shop to mutate into mothers who are rather possessive about their children.* This mutation is especially apparent when women have no salaried work, have no money of their own to play with, misunderstanding their relation to anality, which they see only as a kind of rape, to be encountered and feared as a result of male drives and fantasies. Women see anality as something forced upon them, a kind of anal castration. Their so-called penis—or phallus envy often turns out to be no more than submission to an economic, imaginary, or symbolic organization dictated by the anality and amputation of women necessitated by this economy of the drives and its potential sublimation. Given women's social and cultural role, the commodities that women *are forced to exchange would be their children*, along with the actions and words *related to the children.* Women trade children—with no explicit market organization—in exchange for a market status *for themselves*, insofar as they are objects of value or maternal subjects (?) or function as mothers. In motherhood, women become socially valuable and . . . phallic, according to Freud and others after him. But this phallicism is then of an anal order under different modes, particularly oral modes.

The characteristics of a society organized by exchanges of an anal type are constant whether manufactured products, currency, children, or, to some extent, women are involved. There are substitutive equivalences among these different products. Some are secured by some fixed standard: *procreation.* Others are much more subject to inflation and devaluation. All the fuss about problems of contraception, abortion, and the production of more or less artificial children can be interpreted once it is realized that *the value underpinning our societies for thousands of years has been procreation.* The question is never expressed in these terms, the "work" goes unpaid,[5] the job

5. Here again I have to insist on the symbolic price paid to a woman to bear and give birth to a child for the profit of others. Who, without irony or unconsciousness, can claim that work and working conditions are justly compensated in the face of the derisory sum a woman can earn for bearing and bringing a child into the world? If this payment did not attest to the tragic distress of many women, it would be the funniest response that could be made in objection to the fair pay issue. Equal pay for equal work? What work?

gets wrapped up in some weird kind of holiness, covered with as many masks as there are indispensable repressions and constant misunderstandings. The thing is true for all that.

Any women who are content to let other women feed their children on charity and bear children for nothing are (whether voluntarily or not) full participants in a system of values that prizes sacrifice above all, a system in which children and women have value as commodities that can be relied upon to remain relatively stable, regardless of fluctuations in currencies and economic regimes.

5. Forbidden to celebrate ritual or to participate in social institutions, women are reduced to the polemics and rules of the private sphere. Women are habitually confined to the home and to relations with other women, with children, with mothers and daughters. In this regard, their world seems very like that of certain primitive societies that have no official sacrifices, no recognized rites, no indigenous jurisprudence. Revenge is taken, outside of law or rights, in the form of private attacks, whether concerted or not. In this way a kind of *international vendetta* is set up, virtually in all parts of the world, which prevents the formation of the race of women, the groups and microsocieties that are in the process of coming together. Real murders occur as well as (if the two can be separated) cultural murders, murders of the spirit, the affections, the intelligence, that women perpetuate among themselves.

Certain intellectuals also lack legal status. Their way of life results from the inadequacy of the body of rules that this type of social group accepts.

If social injustice exists in the differences between various work categories as understood by Marx, injustice also occurs in other instances that have received less analysis. Intellectual work is underpaid, even though our societies live off the exploitation of intellectuals who, either directly or indirectly, have given rise to the modes of social and political organization. Thus the intellectual's salary is not paid in the place of work but comes from those who exploit that work. Intellectuals appear to be royal fools when in fact they are kingmakers. Intellectual work is socially dysfunctional: because it is not remunerated in the place where it is produced, it is often subjected to sacrifical misunderstanding. Often recognition comes in old age or posthumously. What is worse, intellectuals write propaganda in favor of the altars on which they will be sacrificed. All this is possible because the value system has not been readjusted to take account of intellectual labor and of women as social resources. *For, if intellectuals are underpaid, women are not paid at all.* Another fundamental aspect of the derangement of our society: there is no recognition that the infrastructure functions for free. No social body can be constituted, developed, or renewed without female labor: without the cathartic function of the beloved mistress or wife, the reproductive function of the mother, the life-giving and caretaking function of the housewife and nurse. This failure to recognize or remember establishes the sacrificial rite or rhythm.

I am putting the two together: intellectuals and women. Their status is linked to an interpretation and an evolution of the mode of thinking and conceiving social organization. All too often that organization is interpreted, imagined, and even programmed only partially, and post hoc. Rarely is any large-scale planning attempted. Perhaps less and less. Only retrospectives are allowed that forget what remains to be discovered, especially the future in the past. The myths and stories, the sacred texts are analyzed, sometimes with nostalgia but rarely with a mind to change the social order. The texts are merely consumed or reconsumed, in a way. The darkness of our imaginary or symbolic horizon is analyzed more or less adequately, but not with the goal of founding a new ethics. The techniques of reading, translating, and explaining take over the domain of the sacred, the religious, the mythical, but they fail to reveal a world that measures up to the material they are consuming or consummating. Work like this, which earns various promotions and credits, is sometimes informative but rarely creative. And thinkers and women do not receive the reward they deserve for providing the dual foundation of social functioning—the united contribution of both mind and nature working at their highest level.

But all thinking that misunderstands its natural roots and resources is not true thinking but rather a threat to life. To discuss or attempt to think about the sublime is valuable providing the sublime respects nature, the micro- and macrocosm, that allows thought to occur. All the rest is mere technocracy, which separates our heads from our bodies or our feet, turning us into ghosts, on the one hand, and machine-serfs, on the other. Women who refuse payment for their work are guilty of the same error.

The money that is not allotted to women in a society like ours upsets the whole social organism. Certain strata or parts of the machinery function on an almost *primitive* level within a highly technocratic whole. Could these small enclaves working in a different way cause the whole society to mutate? Some men and women are gambling that they can. Their gamble is far from being a simple utopia, as others have claimed, but to succeed it relies on a highly rigorous code of ethics that prevents small cells from falling back into the systems they are working against. The gamble will succeed only if the new places that have been set up can be protected from falling back into atopia, exile, while the social scaffolding continues unaffected and swallows up the products of the "primitives," the "mutants," the "rebels," the "others...." Thus society misunderstands differences in order to save (?) the city, maintain (?) order, and make it evolve in cycles that always absorb, digest, and then discard elements that nourish it, which turn over at such speed that the digestion of others can be achieved without the social body suffering poison or death or rebirth.

So is it a matter of killing? That is not the goal. To reveal that murder has been committed means not killing but rather putting an end to the hidden crime, aggression, and sacrifice. This forces the group, or groups, and the individual to find a new balance. To tell someone that he is a criminal, even against his will, is not a punitive act but rather a way to make him conscious of the self and to allow the other to be. Obviously, this changes the economy of consciousness. The masters of the economy no longer have the alibi of helping others because they alone respect the status of some intangible consciousness. The master, or masters, are doubled into two sexes, at least. What is sacrificed is henceforward the all-powerfulness of both one and the other. This new sacrifice opens things up whereas the old immolation habitually led to the creation of a *closed* world through *periodic exclusion*. This new sacrifice, if sacrifice it be rather than a discipline, means that the individual or the social body gives up narcissistic self-sufficiency.

Perhaps that means recognizing that we are still and have always been open to the world and to the other because we are living, sensible beings, subject to the rhythms of time and of a universe whose properties are in part our own, different according to whether we are men or women. Yet for all that we do not have to be members of primitive societies or cultures used to adapting their lives to the fleeting moment, hour, or season in order to respect nature's works and respect ourselves as one of nature's works. Would sacrifice seem vain to us otherwise? Winter is not summer, night is not day, every part of the universe is not equivalent to every other. These rhythms should be enough for us to build societies. Why has man wanted more? Where does man's need to discharge an excess of violence come from? From retarded or arrested growth?

GESTURE IN PSYCHOANALYSIS

Florence, November 2, 1985
Conference organized by the L.A.R.P. at the French Institute:
"The Transmission of Private Experience:
Image, Writing, Voice"

There is very little discussion in psychoanalytic theory of gestures, except in Freud and the early analysts. Today, the issue of physical activity comes up only in therapy for psychotics or children, and in the types of therapy that have moved away from psychoanalysis. Yet it is essential to give some consideration to the movements and gestures that structure the psychoanalytic session. Let me give some examples.

1. One part of the analytic scenario is being expressed by gestures, although this is often neglected in favor of what is being said verbally. The patient is lying on the couch, quite still. The analyst, according to Freud, is also meant to be still and seated. He nonetheless sometimes makes a few small movements. The patient may do so too: he or she may twist a ring, wriggle feet or hands, adopt a conventional position that is far from irrelevant to what he or she is saying. All of this makes a complete statement that must be seen and taken into account. It also forms a whole with the movements of the analyst. The movements of one are motivated by the movements of the other—and this is a two-way street, of course. The analyst often needs to invent some movements that prevent the two subjective economies, his own and the patient's, from becoming intertwined.

At one point I had planned to address this question exclusively. I had thought I might explain why knitting or doing needlework as one listened to a patient were topologically intelligent and subtle activities that preserved the freedom of both partners in the act. It has taken me years to discover this and begin to interpret it. I had also planned to describe to you a certain number of discoveries about gestures that I had made, which led to certain successful therapeutic outcomes. The whole thing is fascinating! But would this place you and me in an unethical position? In effect, I would have been acting out my work as an analyst, showing in public something that I believe should remain secret. This is a difficult issue. For years, it has prevented me from writing a book about the psychoanalytical clinic. I have asked my patients if they would like to collaborate with me in writing up their analyses. This did not produce great results! Perhaps they wanted to keep their secrets? Some of my male and female patients have written for themselves, without even mentioning the name of their analyst in most cases. It is true that I am a woman. Which must partly explain why I am not cited. Thus I have only recently decided to offer a few fragments of my psychoanalytic practice in the special issue of the journal *Langages* devoted to language and sex.[1] In this article, I merely looked at the structure of language and its communication schemas. This form of interpretation seems to me a way of bringing to public notice certain transferential mechanisms, and to deflate the power that analysis owes to the silence observed about its practice. All this without, however, betraying patient confidence. In fact I doubt if my patients recognize themselves in the very short extracts I have published from their transcripts.

In order to respect the ethics of psychoanalysis and above all to maintain faith with my patients, I shall therefore refer to certain movements and actions that occur in every analysis. Let me start with two essential positions taken up on the analytic stage that analysis took over from hypnosis: *one person (originally the woman) is lying down, the other person is sitting down, and facing the back of the first person's head.* These two parameters—sitting at someone's back, and lying down—disobey not only social convention but also the relation of signs to language. In fact, these last are produced in a position orthogonal to the choice and constitution of their meaning. The position adopted in psychoanalysis prevents them from being produced in this manner. What makes the patient annoyed and nervous when he or she is lying down is first of all the impossibility of producing an exact word or meaning *that relates to the here and now.* This stage has been set for *remembering.* The patient recalls something, or rambles, or he confides the truth of the work he is producing to the analyst while lying at right angles to the analyst.[2] But the patient is also unable to address a current *message* since the identity of the speaker and the person spoken to, of the world, or even of the subject, of the addressee, of the object, have not been fixed. Therefore the economy of discourse and communication is

1. See "L'Ordre sexuel du discours," *Langages* (March 1987), no. 85, pp. 81–123.
2. See, in this regard, my essay "Le praticable de la scene" in *Parler n'est jamais neutre* (Paris: Minuit, 1985).

disrupted. After hypnosis, Freud placed the patient, originally a woman, in a situation of *immersion* insofar as language and relations of known exchanges are concerned. From the onset of the sessions, or sessions, the patient was dislocated from his habits as a speaking subject, from his system of representational, social, and familial relations. . . . He is not really hypnotized but immersed in language and in his own history, which changes into something both other and like himself (a horizon, a territory, a veil, clouds, an ocean . . .) that he does not know. And he or she is unable to easily build bridges or platforms that would allow escape because he is deprived of the power *in the present* of producing *rational* speech. It is not surprising that the position asked of patients in psychoanalysis is experienced as an aggression. That is exactly what it is. On the other hand, if the analyst knows his or her business, the position does not represent the same seizure of power as in hypnosis. The position is necessary if the patient is to cross back into his language. The patient has come into analysis because he or she is in pain. Analysis forbids the patient to simulate normalcy, assuming that exists. The patient is held still so that his speech can be reconstituted in another way. And in speech I include gestures. Obviously this is not a question of teaching the subject a new code, doctrine, etc., but of helping him or her to structure a new house of language, as Heidegger has noted. It is probably to this conception of the link between the subject and language that Jacques Lacan owes his definition of the unconscious. The phrase "The unconscious is structured like a language" is very close to this passage by Martin Heidegger: "Man acts as though he were the shaper and master of language, while in fact language remains the master of man."[3]

2. So the psychoanalytic scenario involves gestures that are foreign to any other situation. Is this *gestural system* the same for men and women? Is it identical between different sexes? Depending upon whether the analyst is of the same sex as the patient or the other? No. Why? In the first place there is a very simple reason: lying down does not have the same sexual connotation for a man and a woman. It is relatively common for a man, in an erotic situation, to tell a woman to lie down, or to lay her down. This social habit in fact leads to a certain number of rapes of analysands by analysts. It is much rarer, it is in fact exceptional, for a woman to ask a man to lie

3. See Heidegger, "Man Lives as a Poet," in *Poetry, Language, Thought*, p. 215.

down, except in therapy. Between persons of the same sex, the connotations are much more blurred.

The analytic setup, which has a strong influence on the discourse and the communication achieved in the session, does not work *neutrally*. It carries sexual variants depending upon the partners. The patients have a sex, have a past and a present as sexual beings, as does the analyst. Yet it appears that the high priests of sexuality take very little account of sex in their professional outlook. Is this puritanical attitude left over from religion? Is it a result of lack of information? For example, many psychoanalysts ignore the fact that men and women do not have the same number of bodily orifices: in men urine and semen use the same channel, but this is not true for women. This fact has many heavy erotic consequences, which occasion repression and create errors in the attribution of corporal identity. This may also be a case of lack of sexual imaginary, or of misplaced idealism. In contemporary society, the stress on the neuter/neutral seems to me linked to the cultural mood of a technological era that likes to think in terms of a neutral energy that can compete with and mimic the machine. This energy is ultimately located in God even though he has never been neuter in our traditions since the inauguration of monotheism.

3. One argument put forward in defense of making no sexual distinctions is that analysis creates a return to *childedness*. This is my own word, and it brings me to the third issue I want to raise today: *Is the child neuter?* Is the child said to be neuter because—as I have heard some people claim—the word for child is neuter in German, the language of Freud? This seems to me to be a very weak argument! It is also tragic, in the sense in which Hegel talks about the tragic in the constitution of the ethical order, tragic in the sense of the great tragedies that mark the beginning of our sociocultural order. Even the child or already the child is considered to be neuter or neutered before he or she begins to speak! What a loss of freedom in the imaginary, the symbolic, in nonverbal expression. I wonder, incidentally, why analysts have recourse to bilingualism when discussing the bilingual therapy that Anna O. invented for herself. Unable to express themselves in their own language, these analysts have recourse to another language. This device is forced upon them to ward off aphasia and paralysis. The problem in this case as in many others is that this autotherapeutic symptom becomes a truth norm.

Perhaps it is relevant to understand this move to assign the neuter gender to childhood as yet one more result of the technological era we live in and that psychoanalysis also partakes in. If its practioners do not take care, analysis becomes merely a school of technocratic orthodoxy for our unconscious. Now machines are intended to present themselves as more or less neuter. The truth of machines is supposed to be as neutral as that of currency. Our technical world claims to be neuter, though nature has always had a sex.

The two hypotheses I have just offered are not incompatible. This means that, instead of an aphasia or a paralysis, a model is set up that takes the place of a prosthesis. This model is all the more rigid because it has been amputated from its living subjective symptomatology. The *one* of the model or its *anyone* or *everyone*, its claim to be *true*, etc., are necessarily much more rigid than the symptoms of Anna O. Her symptoms, as I listen to them, have much more energy and theoretical potential and their hieroglyphics have yet to be fully decoded.

4. But let us get back to the child and investigate whether the child is neuter. To answer that question, I return to the scene that, acccording to Freud, marks the entry into the symbolic order. The example he gives is of his grandson Ernst playing with a reel on the end of a string while his mother is absent. The child throws the reel away from him to a place where it is hidden and then pulls it toward him saying *o-o-o-o* and *da*, which is interpreted as *fort-da*. He throws it onto the bed, where it is hidden, and he pulls it back, in full visibility, out of the bed. *Fort* means far, *da* means near. *Fort* (or *o-o-o-o*, as it is signaled discontinuously) plays, in the economy of consonants and vowels, on the far-near: its articulation sets up the mouth in a little triangle with the lips and the tongue: the *o* is inside but cannot be swallowed. The far is not introjected but it sketches, especially in the mouth, a demarcated space, a frame. This frame constitutes a kind of two-way space braked by the *t*, if the word is *fort*, or by the discontinuity in the sound if it is *o-o-o-o*. The *da*, on the other hand, can be completed in one brisk swallow, inverting the *fort*, unless it is held at the back of the palate. So everything again happens in the mouth: between the lips, the tongue, the palate, the teeth, the larynx, the potential confusion of larynx with esophagus, the uncertainty between esophagus, larynx, and pharynx, etc. *Da* is not sung, in any case, it is swallowed. From close up, it is introjected: far away, it is mastered: it is held in the mouth like a hard

candy or else becomes a discontinuous signal, hard to transform into a melody, remaining a kind of syncopated rhythm lacking something necessary for the constitution of a closed object. This almost-thing is physically laid in the bed. It is supposed to live there, hidden, until the boy calls it. *Da* has to be jerked back, otherwise the reel stays where it is, and is swallowed or hangs at the back of the palate without the to-and-fro game. *Da* goes down, or not, but it is more inside you than is *fort*, and is closed off by the teeth.

Both *fort* and *da* are stopped by the teeth. Whereas the reel comes and goes, and the arm (probably the right arm) moves, the breath and the meaning are in the power of the teeth. The mother is held back behind the teeth. She is unable to get out, in any event. She is held back in readiness to become articulation *(fort)* or else she is inside, swallowed or blocking the throat at the back of the palate *(da)*. She does not get out of the mouth. Not only is she in the bed but also in the mouth, behind the teeth. She is located in two places, outside and inside. But on the inside she is already divided infinitely by the teeth and all the differences between the sounds.

This is the action of Ernst, of a little boy whose mother is away, an action designed to master that absence, according to Freud. In *French* we don't seem to have the same articulation of syllables, and things therefore work out less successfully, the positions are even reversed. Freud writes in German, moreover he is Jewish, which means that, for him, the vowel-consonant opposition has a special importance. We have to keep Freud's culture and language clearly in mind and not blindly transpose a model built in one language onto another language. What would be the corresponding model for a little boy who spoke French? Is there one? What syllables express it? Would the French child have said *ici* and *la?* These words do not correspond to the same positions in the mouth as the German words. *Fort* seems to stand somewhere between the French *la* and *ici*. Moreover the *a* sound is associated with outside and it is the vowel *i* plus *s* that will express the *da*. *Ici* is pronounced in the front of the mouth, lips open with a head vowel: *i*. The change in language has not invalidated the hypothesis that the child's actions express appropriation, it has merely questioned it.

What I wanted to point out in relation to the story of Ernst is that neither we nor Freud usually interpret the fact that it is with a gesture of the hand and arm, accompanied by certain spoken syllables, that the little boy masters the absence of his mother and is thus able to enter the symbolic universe. What happens later to those meshed articulations of arm and sound-making apparatus? And another question: is Ernst walking or stationary when he performs the *fort-da?* Probably he is not walking. He is not using his legs to find his mother. Why? Why does he stay still, as if his legs were paralyzed? He looks for his mother with arm and mouth. Perhaps with ears too? Sounds vibrate in his mouth and reverberate in his ears. To some extent, he talks to himself. Certain sounds are made as if the mouth were pronouncing them toward the outside, others as if for the self, vibrating in the inner ear membranes. The *da* is spoken toward the inside. It starts out on the outside and is spoken inside. The *a* is more maternal as well, more ancient, more enveloping. While listening to himself, Ernst may be listening to his mother, and drinking her in with the *da.* In any case, it is as if Ernst is driving a car or a tank. He drives something with his mouth, his string, and his reel, that relate to his mother, his bed, his word. It should be added that his second game, in the absence of the mother, is to make himself appear or disappear in a mirror.

Ernst is a boy. When I raised this question of Ernst's maleness one day at a Cerisy conference (cf. "Belief Itself," in this volume), someone objected that Ernst could have been a girl. My answer was: he was a boy. It is important to be faithful to the text. Not every substitution is possible, especially when sexual difference is involved. In Freud's text, then, the child is a boy. And Freud never wrote that it might have been a girl. My hypothesis is that it couldn't have been a girl. Why? A girl does not do the same things when her mother goes away. She does not play with a string and a reel that symbolize her mother, because her mother is of the same sex as she is and cannot have the object status of a reel. The mother is of the same subjective identity as she is.

So what will the girl's reactions be? 1) When she misses her mother, she throws herself down on the ground in distress, she is lost, she loses the power and the will to live, she neither speaks nor eats, totally anorexic. 2) She plays with a doll, lavishing maternal affection on a quasi subject, and thus manages to organize a kind of symbolic space; playing with dolls is not simply a game girls are forced to play, it also signifies a difference in subjective status in the separation from the mother. For mother and daughter, the mother is a subject that cannot easily be reduced to an object, and a doll is not an object in the way that a reel, a toy car, a gun, etc., are objects and tools used for symbolization. 3) She dances and thus forms a vital subjective space open to the cosmic maternal world, to the gods, to the present other. This dance is also a way for the girl to create a territory of her own in relation to the mother.

Does the girl speak? If she does, it is in a playful mode, without any special attention to oppositions of syllables and phonemes. It can be bisyllabic or like a litany or song, tonally modulated. This language corresponds to a rhythm but also to a melody. Sometimes it finds expression in words of tenderness or anger addressed to the doll, sometimes by silence.

Among women, the relationship to sameness and to the mother is not mastered by the *fort-da*. The mother always remains too familiar and too close. In a way, the daughter has her mother under her skin, secreted in the deep, damp intimacy of the body, in the mystery of her relationship to gestation, to birth, and to her sexual identity. Furthermore, the sexual movement characteristic of the female is whirling round rather than throwing and pulling objects back as little Ernst does. The girl tries to reproduce around and within her an energetic circular movement that protects her from abandonment, attack, depression, loss of self. Spinning round is also, but in my opinion secondarily, a way of attracting. The girl describes a circle while soliciting and refusing access to her territory. She is making a game of this territory she has described with her body. There is no object here, in the strict meaning of the word, no other that has had to be introjected or incorporated. On the contrary, girls and women often set up a defensive territory that can then become creative, especially in analysis.

Graphic examples of the shape of these territories are given by Jung, who compares them to Tibetan mandelas. In these drawings it appears also that the girl, the woman, is not calling the other back, as Ernst does with his reel; she is calling the other to her and playing with the borders that give access to the territory where she stands.

If the mother—and girls' identities in relation to her—is invoked in girls' play, and if they choose to play with a cord, they skip around, while turning the cord over their bodies. You must have all seen girls playing with jump ropes in the school yard. They describe a circular territory around themselves, around their bodies. It is quite a different movement from Ernst's. Sometimes girls whirl around in silence or else they giggle, and chatter, and chant nursery rhymes. Perhaps chant is not quite the right word: they make up variants, invent phonic and syllabic games.

Girls do not enter into language in the same way as boys. If they are too worn down with grief they never speak at all. Otherwise they enter language by producing a space, a path, a river, a dance, a rhythm, a song. . . . Girls describe a space around themselves rather than displacing a substitute object from one place to another or into various places; clearly visible in the hand, invisible in the bed, in the mouth in front of or behind the tongue, in the throat, etc. Girls keep everything and nothing. That is their mystery, their attraction. Of course they do play with distance, but in another way. They interiorize the greatest distances without dichotomic alternations, except that *they whirl about in different directions:* toward the outside, toward the inside, on the border between the two. They whirl not only toward or around an external sun but also around themselves and within themselves. The *fort-da* is not their move into language. It is too linear, too analogous with the to-and-fro of the penile thrust or its manual equivalent, with the mastery of the other by means of an object, it is too angular also. Girls enter into language without taking anything inside themselves (except perhaps the void?). They do not speak about an introjected him or introjected her, but talk *with* (sometimes in) a silence and with the other-mother in any case. Girls can find no substitutes for the mother except the whole of nature, the call to the divine or to do likewise. Woman always speaks *with* the mother, man speaks in her absence. This *with her* obviously takes different shapes and it must seek to place speech *between,* not to remain in an indissociable fusion, with the women woven together. This *with* has to try to become a *with self.* Mother and daughter turn around each other, they go up and down while encircling themselves but they also delineate the two entities that they are: in the lips, the hands, the eyes.

The girl-subject does not exert mastery, except perhaps in her silence, her becoming, her overflowing. The girl-subject does not have objects as the boy does. It splits into two in a different way and the object or the goal is to reunite the two by a gesture, to touch both perhaps so that birth is repeated, so that no unconsidered regression occurs, so that the self is kept whole or, sometimes, upright. Women do not try to master the other but to give birth to themselves. They only stoop to mastering the other (the child, for example, insofar as they have the power) when they are unable to engender their own axis and lose the freedom to be engendered. Their axis is also or again the one that passes through the feet and goes up to the crown of the head as well as further down and further up. Their absolute need is not for penis or phallus but for the chance to be born to themselves, to find autonomy, to be free to *walk*, walk away and walk back, however it pleases them. The need for the phallus that has been attributed to women is an a posteriori justification for the obligation laid on women to become legal wives and mothers. Their need is for an axis of their own, which on the microcosmic level moves from between the feet in the standing position up through the head, and macrocosmically from the center of the earth to the center of the sky. This axis can be seen represented in the iconographic traces of traditions in which women had some visible presence. This is how women find the necessary conditions to establish their territory and the autonomy of their body and their flesh, with a growing potential to enjoy sexual pleasure (*jouissance*). Women's pleasure does not demand that they isolate an arm or a hand in order to master the other; they keep all their limbs, all the body in movement, especially their legs. It is interesting to note that the paralysis of female hysterics described by Freud and Breuer affects the *legs*. Paralysis strikes in different ways, depending upon whether the trauma is recent or longstanding, and, sometimes, upon whether the author of the trauma is a man or a woman. This is well described by Freud and Breuer. Nonetheless, I am not happy with the interpretation they give of hysterical paralysis. In my opinion, the pain comes from the loss of, or inability to achieve, autoeroticism, which the female body expresses differently from the male, just as the female's access to language differs from the male's. The actions are different, as are the words.

It could be that girls keep their *lips closed* as a positive move. The positive meaning of closed lips does not rule out singing or talking. It expresses a difference. Girls have less need to master the absence of the mother. But they may still choose to be silent and close the lips, keep the lips, the labials, as threshold to the mouth, the labials as opposed to the *dentals*, using the whole of the lips, not just the corners. If women sing, they generally use the whole of the lips, and not just the corners, as in *fort-da, ici* or *la*. . . . The importance of the lips corresponds to that of the generation of the universe, but already in silence. Certain traditions, notably the tantric tradition, teach us this. These same traditions tell us that, to designate something that is not yet manifest, you should say *m*, keeping the lips closed in a hum. The word to designate mother often includes the letter *m*. In French, *maman* means, at least phonetically, that which is kept but which cannot be represented, expressed, mastered, that which suspends consumption but favors respiration, that which covers the whole with a vast blackness expressed by the *m* and potentially matches all colors thanks to the *a*. This name is one of the most perfect words possible.

I have read in a book by René Guénon called *Les symboles de la science sacrée* (Paris: Gallimard, 1962) that the etymology of the word *labyrinth, labrys,* is still unclear. Guénon suggests that *labyrinth* is derived from *lapis,* stone, or shares the same root. My hypothesis is that the word has the same etymology as lips: *labra,* plural of *labrum.* The labyrinth, whose path was known to Ariadne, for example, would thus be that of the lips. This mystery of the female lips, they way they open to give birth to the universe, and touch together to permit the female individual to have a sense of her identity, would be the forgotten secret of perceiving and generating the world. Freud often reduces female neurosis to the oral stage and especially the labial, and yet, though he is far from lacking culture and archeological lore, he makes nothing of the cultural tradition relating to lips. Of course, that tradition is largely oriental and Christian: the gestures of the Virgin are close to those of the yogis of the East. But, in Jewish tradition there are times when the lips are shown as a reversed double *yod,* a double reversed tongue.[4] This same design is used for the holy spirit when it hovers in the shape of a bird over the earth and the seas. Thus it signifies the creative spirit that moved over the waters when, by his word, God created the heaven and the earth.

I believe that by forgetting the importance of the lips, a labyrinthine omission has been opened up in the deciphering of the universe and language, just as an enigma has been lodged in the interpretation of sexual difference. The origin of this omission seems to be associated with those traditions in which men have taken over divine power, stealing that dimension of generative potential (*puissance*) from women and from the cosmic. The men gods, or certain ones at least, the man god of monotheism, creates the universe and all that it contains of life through his word: in the case of man, he also uses hand and breath. This world, their world, seems at first sight discontinuous, divided almost dichotomously. Yet the universe does not obey an intermittent rhythm but rather traces a continuous

4. See *The Symbolic Animals of Christianity* by Louis Charbonneau-Lassay, London: Stewart and Watkins, 1970, p. 106.

growth made up of blossoming and dying down, expanding and cutting back, flowering and putting down roots.

The enigma of woman would largely reside in the enigma of her lips and all they keep unmanifested. This would explain the reaction of Dora—and many of her sisters in similar situations—when Herr K. tried to kiss her. There is, in my view, no need to invent a theory of pathological displacement. The lips of themselves represent a sufficiently important place of cathexis that a kiss becomes a kind of rape, not to be supported easily. To take a woman's lips would be like taking a man's *fort-da*. In fact it is worse. The *fort-da* is already a substitutional mechanism, whereas the lips are the woman herself, the threshold to a woman that has not been distanced by any object. Stealing a woman's kiss is to take the most virginal part of her, the part most linked to her female identity. To get a woman with child is another rape, the transgression of another threshold. To force a woman to speak, while she is lying down, what's more, can amount to therapeutic rape. The woman is not protected by the mechanism of the *fort-da*, and the way it sets up division—of time, of space, of the other, of the self, its mechanism of phonetic fractions. A woman can usually find self-expression only when her lips are touching together and when her whole body is in movement. A woman is more at a loss when she is still than when she is moving, because when fixed in one position she is a prisoner, open to attack in her own territory.

5. If I might make one last remark today about gesture on the psychoanalytic stage, let me raise the issue of the opposition virgin-paranoiac, of Dora and Schreber, the couple who stand at the origins of analytic practice. Schreber's persecution mania is built upon the notion that he is a virgin made fruitful by the rays of the father God. But this delirium of virginity between men is possible only when his wife is absent, or more generally when women are absent. Yet, oddly enough, he dedicates the story of his mania to his wife. I interpret this to mean that, because women have not been allowed to keep their gestures, their imaginary, their symbols, these things become lodged like foreign bodies in the verbal (in the widest sense) imaginary of man. Instead of a marriage, a nuptial union that can also be cultural, there is on the one hand a virgin who has become a real mother and nothing more, and on the other a man, a real father who raves about being a virgin impregnated by God in the absence of his wife. The symbol of sexual difference and its fertility have been lost.

Whereas they once had been fertile together in the spirit, man and woman lose their divinity and the fulfillment of their humanity. The forms that, according to some Eastern and even Christian traditions, once emanated from the woman's lips, turn into those piercing rays of light that enter Schreber and supposedly link him to God. My belief is that in fact they belong rather to the lost imaginary of his wife and its own economy. That which has not been engendered by his wife and has been reduced to mere real motherhood becomes a persecution mania for Schreber. He, like Ernst, played with movements and words, with his image in the mirror, in order to make up for the absence of his mother. In these substitutions, he seeks to master the whole of her, including the woman's virginity that is invisible yet present especially in the specular processes of self-production or reproduction. It seems to me that, before invoking God as cause, we must rather work on being fully sexed beings, which would include recognizing the creative character of female sexuality in its biological forms and resources—things that other traditions have respected. But Schreber, instead of becoming fully a man, particularly in his symbolic creativity, becomes a woman or tries to borrow the virginal sex of his wife while she is far away and he can surround himself with medical personnel.

This strange couple, composed of a woman who is paralyzed in her body and a man who raves of the female imaginary instead of fulfilling the work of his body, is still with us today. The rape of Dora as well as her phobias, paralyses, and ensuing hysterias are the counterpart of Screber's mania. Woman's micro- and macrocosmic universe often serves as a theoretical and practical mania for man, as an abstract system that has been uprooted from the rhythms and regulations of the body. Where there was birth and natural and vegetal cycles there is now a construction of artificial cultures with strange gods, strange stars, labyrinthine and cryptomanic laws full of terrors and taboos, and excessive, pathogenic, orderless pleasures. Everything turns neurotic and violent, in need of doctors and medication. Inner and outer perceptions seem lost.

As some people have said—Lacan, for example—the scene of analysis is always threatened by paranoia. My interpretation is that that threat comes from not perceiving or respecting the virginity of woman and the resulting inflation of the male's imaginary world as he takes over this mystery into his language, his mirror, and deceives himself. This mystery, to sum up, is a creative economy of the senses. Once removed from its roots, stripped of its style, this economy hardens, grows rigid, turns into crypts and arrows, waves of pain and manic delusions of giving birth. Dora and Schreber, in their respective sufferings, can help us to see the reasons for their illness and give us some part of what they, and we, need to recover.

THE FEMALE GENDER

Rotterdam, November 14, 1985
Conference at Erasmus University:
"The Other and Thinking About Difference"

A machine has no sex. Nature, on the other hand, always has a sex. Obviously there are times when a machine mimics sex. And, moreover, machinery is more akin to one sex than the other, particularly in its status as tool. The machine, which is produced to have either no sex or one single sex, does at times protect and assist life. But it never creates or engenders life.

The human spirit already seems subjugated to the imperatives of technology to the point of believing it possible to deny the difference of the sexes. Anyone who stresses the importance of sexual difference is accused of living in the past, of being reactionary or naive, even though science is far from having come up with all the answers about sex. Some men and women really do live in the past. But, as long as we are still living, we are sexually differentiated. Otherwise, we are dead. The question of whether language has a sex could be subtitled: *Are we still alive? alive enough to rise above the level of a machine, a mechanism, to exert an energy that escapes the mastery of the subject?* Are we alive enough to create, engender life, form, spirit? If we are to remain alive and regenerate ourselves as living beings, we need sexual difference.

From the point of view of the mind or spirit, this difference seems to be a real contradiction: no ill-placed complementarity, no acquired objective position, whether of object or image. There is a physiological and morphological complementarity between the sexes. Why deny it? This complementarity should be lived in such a way as to facilitate growth. But in our becoming there has been no sexual difference established on the level of the *subject*. This is the opportunity that still lies before us, particularly in our thinking.

We are in the process of passing into another environment, which, for many people, replaces the natural one. For many of us today the technological milieu necessarily becomes the normal, everyday environment. Where once we had earth, sun, plant life, water, air, there is now concrete, electricity, air conditioning, train, plane, stations, gas pumps. . . . Quite apart from the difference in what we are given to see, smell, feel, taste, there is the noise factor—noise that can be punctuated by clocks, according to a rhythm that certain bands are trying to copy. But it is a crazy noise because it is no longer ruled by the seasons or the landscape, for example. The noise of the machine varies little according to the seasons, the regions or the countries of the world. There is more or less of it, but it is almost always the same. Does this cause a regression in our perceptions? Today we alternate, if at all, between noise and silence. But silence does not exist. This alternation is artificial and obscene. The real alternation should be between the noise of the machine and the noise of nature. Nature's noise is rhythmic. What's more, it respects the differences in rhythms. It *informs*. It is always a one-time occurrence. It is always *damp* also, that is to say capable of touching without inflicting harm. The noise of the machine is always the same. This is in fact the condition of its efficiency. It works by repetition. The machine is to be trusted only if it repeats. When it ceases to be able to repeat, it is flawed, broken. Nature, on the other hand, does not repeat. It is in continuous becoming. Even when similarities in her cycles occur, nature never repeats herself identically. She grows, becomes, joining together the root and the flower. She endlessly informs, through sound and all the other sensations.

Nature has a sex, always and everywhere. All traditions that remain faithful to the cosmic have a sex and take account of natural powers (*puissances*) in sexual terms. They are also regulated by alternations that do not truly contradict each other. Spring is not autumn nor summer winter, night is not day. This is not the opposition that we know from logic in which the one is opposed to or contradicts the other, where the one is superior to the other and *must put the inferior down*. There is a rhythm of growth in which both poles are necessary, or so it seems. Winter does not destroy summer, it allows the sap to flow down into the earth and take new root. Can we imagine the sap remaining eternally fecond at the top of the tree? This is not sure. Nature tells us the opposite. But, apparently, men have forgotten this lesson. Man seems to go to the top and stay there and leave the others, women for example, to occupy the low ground, while the path between heaven and earth is lost. In any case they forget that they are obliged to go back down to their roots if they are to grow. They remain now and forever nostalgic for their first roots in the mother, but the immediacy of that nostalgia is killed or contradicted. This does not solve the problem, however.

These swings between treetops and roots show up again in *the culture's movements up and down* and in *wars*.

War, which is sometimes the only conceivable way out of technical expansion, would be the *negation of negation*. Does this mean that war is a *return to the immediacy of the senses?* Instead of cultivating the senses as his own heritage, as the nature of his spirit, man—or, more specifically, the *race of men*—seems to dissociate himself from them and leave them to the other of nature, the other gender in particular. In public, it is true, man only wants to wage war on his own gender: the other war is meant to remain hidden, secret, as if it had been resolved upon in absolute knowledge and spirit. Which is not true. The fulfilled spirit also appears as a negation of negation. The spirit, in its perfection, also signifies the return of that which has been denied or not dialecticized as immediate in sensual experience. Does the absolute character of sensation make a comeback in the absolute of conception? The absolute is the other name for the immediate—at least for man. The absolute is the nostalgic and all-enveloping return of the senses into knowledge, and of knowledge into the senses. The absolute is goal and horizon, the aim and the masked passage from the sensual into the mental, and its return in the shape of a topological whole, of a potentially closed universe. It would achieve another world, a double of the world, a made-to-measure, uprooted world, were it not for the tragedy of the two genders. But the absolute, unlike the most probable cosmic rhythm, kills, saps vitality, because it tears nature away from temporalization. Or at least this is the risk that can be observed in its relation to gender. The spirit, in its perfection, does not thrust its roots deeper into the earth. It destroys its first roots. Its soil has become culture, history, which successfully forget that anything that conceives has its origins in the flesh.

But, despite what some cultures and religions predict, the dead are not resuscitated as such. If they do return to life it is in a world other than that of absolute spirit, a world of different senses. As for the earth, it is woman's role to lay the dead there, if she has not been stripped of this ethical duty.

The male gender, usually called the human race, plays a game with its other but never couples with it, and ends up by forgetting its gender and destroying its sexual roots. Perhaps it deteriorates and prefers to suffer decline, pain, and death rather than encounter the other. He and all his avatars would be possible, but not the other. Why? To want the absolute is not to want those frustrations, privations, temperings that occur when we renounce the immediate for the self so as to secure the work of the negative in the relationship with the other. The absolute knowledge of *one* subject, of *one* gender is in fact the sign that the work of the negative has not been completed. A god of flesh and sex has more to say to the acceptance of the work of the negative, the need to take a body if one is to become divine and accede to perfection. Would a couple god have more to say, and more dialectically yet? No man or woman would achieve absolute knowledge within or according to his or her gender. Each would be constituted in time through a constant articulation between the genders, a dialectic between two figures or incarnations of the living that are represented in sexual difference, and there alone.

☆

The issues of women's liberation and of the affirmation of a different identity often skirt the real ethical tragedy facing us. Hegel had some perception of this and predicted or diagnosed the fact that the ethical order was heading precipitously down, especially in the unresolved opposition between human law and divine law, each allotted respectively as duty (and destiny?) to man and to woman. The division of roles Hegel thus establishes seems very odd in a world where the divine has already been taken away from the female and is now the province of the male gender, even in respect to the guardianship of the family, of living being, of the gods. In place of a fully realized dialectic between the spiritual duties of both genders, Hegel presents us with a *doubly locked closing*. This constitutes the strength of his system, which no one, in my view, has managed to unlock.

Why is this system fastened with at least double locks? Because the female has been buried together with the divine law in that woman presides over nature and gender, protects the family and respects the cult of the dead. But the practice of that law, which Antigone was the last to perform, already bears the stamp of the male universe. Antigone is no longer a woman protecting the light, the hearth fire, its gods, its life, she is a woman who palliates the destruction of the family wrought by the conflict of two brothers, both of whom seek power over the people. Already Antigone is working in the service of the god of men and of their *pathos*. She tries to make up for their crime, to brush error aside so as to appease the

110

gods of the dead and leave the living with no trace of crime. It is no longer a case of her fulfilling her role as a member of the *female gender*. Antigone already serves the state in that she tries to wipe away the blood shed by the state in its bid for power and human rights through *sacrifice*. Thus the female has already ceased to serve her own gender, her dialectic. The female has been taken along, taken in by the passage out of divine law, out of the law of nature, of life, into male human law. Antigone is already the desexualized representative of *the other of the same*. Faithful to her task of respecting and loving the home, careful not to pollute the hearth flame, she now performs only the dark side of that task, the side needed to establish the male order as it moves toward absolute affirmation. When engaged in redressing her brothers' crime, Antigone is no longer fulfilling her own task, her *affirmative* relationship to ethics, she no longer serves *her* gods. The female gender, in its singularity, has been lost in this character who resists but nonetheless submits, out of womanly—or maternal?—fidelity to the male gods and to war among men. Antigone is no longer a *goddess*. She keeps faith with the gods of the shadows of men, and she dies as a result. In order to wipe a stain away once more. What stain? Fundamentally, the stain of her consciousness, of belonging to the female race, of having a maternal filiation. Eliminated because of this doubly clandestine membership of the female gender, Antigone is also annihilated because she keeps faith with the lost roots of man.

The split in the concept takes place within sameness; but, in the concept the split remains that of the female and of the male. Language tends to reverse that split. It keeps the *marker* for the feminine while leaving the masculine as matter, as the habitual substance of language that lies beneath the marker and above, as absolute spirit or as God. The male becomes the substrate for the encircling whole and the source that ensures it. The opposite takes place: the female remains the source, the substrate, the encircling whole and *the male is the marker* that knows nothing of nature (including phonics, phonetics, linguistics) and nothing of the female gender as nature. The concept has two heroes. But one of them is reduced to a marker, an inappropriate mask, a hypothetical garment, the other is supposed to become matter, subject, the encircling absolute. *Language reverses all that the dialectic describes—and reciprocally.* The circle is closed by this blind dialectical reversal in discourse. Language is the *tool* of the universal. Yet it is not the universal. Anything associated with nature is immediately universal; that which passes through articulation is only mediately universal. Among its various vocations this universal aims to destroy the spirit of the family, the spirit of sex. The universal tool wants citizens who are *neuter* in regard to familial singularity, its laws, and *necessary sexual difference*. The demand for the *equality* of the sexes often forms a part of this plan to neuter familial and sexual singularity for the benefit of the State and its laws, a plan that includes the materialist reversals of this era of ours, which is devoted to the technical. Yet these laws have openly sacrificed woman and covertly sacrificed man.

The aim of the family is singular, individual, but not the contingent individual, the future citizen who will cease to belong to the family. The aim of the family, of gender, of sexuality, is the individual as universal, the *daimon*, the soul or the individual that are denied as contingent. This noncontingent individual is traditionally the province of woman, guardian of gender. The theoretical or practical fact of defining women as parts of a whole (one female + one female + one female ...) is a way of not recognizing their own gender, their individuality with a universal vocation. Women correspond to the *universal singular*. In themselves, they unite the most singular to the most universal. *Their identity consists in the systematic nonsplit of nature and spirit, in the touching together of these two universals.* Woman is whole and universal, universal if whole. Here again our culture has inverted the order of things; which explains how the spirit has become alien to itself. Women are or remain more *daimon*, that is, noncontingent individuals, than men. This is so not only for the *mother* but for *woman already*. The kind of worship that is rendered to woman is not necessarily, and in fact in our culture rarely—except in the usually misunderstood cult of *virginity*—addressed to this *daimon* that woman is as natural and universal, as nature and spirit not radically split.

Clearly, according to Hegel, the dead man is the one who finally finds peace. He is no longer internally split, no longer in constant *polemos*. But it might be possible to have another peace: that of living plant growth. The ensemble of the Hegelian system, apart from a few errors and uprootings, in fact resembles this. Could the secret model for his philosophy overall be *the plant?* But, within the system, as it unfolds on the conscious level, it seems that one can escape from singularness only through the order of death or of the dead man. This idea or conviction seems linked to the *split of body and spirit* that is established following the sacrifice of the female to the State and man's access to citizenship and to a neutered culture.

In fact it is possible to go beyond singularness by obeying growth, by sharing in the universal natural rhythm. This sharing is indeed more universal than a single death. Obviously, the universality of nature is complex, but it is ceaselessly *a figure both complete and changing,* finished and open, globally peaceful in its achievements. Because it refuses any debt to the family and its sexualized relation to life, the being of nature that has become immediate is death. Because it refuses any debt to nature, the return to nature can only be of the order of death.

There is more: once the natural, familial, female, or, if you like, nocturnal spirit, is sacrificed, the dark rootedness of nature is rejected in favor of a *sightless era of concepts.* This sightlessness seems to consist in the unconsidered, unconscious destruction of our senses. Having annihilated the *pour-soi* of consciousness, men, or *the race of men destroy the en-soi of the world of the senses and its way of becoming en-soi pour soi.* This destruction risks reducing or even annihilating the contents of the spirit. It seems that little thought is given to the senses as such in the development of the spirit, attention not to the *pathos* of the spirit but to *sense perception* as matter or substance for the spirit. Open, declared warfare destroys the people, but it also serves to distract the consciousness from noting another more hidden war that leads to the destruction of the the world of the senses as possible content for the spirit. It lures the consciousness away from caring about the impact of noise upon our bodily equilibrium, for example. War, both past and future, tears consciousness away from its duty to prevent nature from being destroyed, along with the food and shelter of life. Yet this hidden destruction also leads to war, to blind violence, to famine.

The race of men feigns to be all innocence because it represents (or claims to represent?) the light side of the spirit. Men repress the other side. They smile politely *as if only doing their duty* as they wound or kill. They are unconscious of evil, at least at the time they are perpetrating it, and lay claim to absolute consciousness all the while as a kind of tool to buckle culture up with. But must one, must I, leave the unconscious every right, every excuse? My response, even as a practicing psychoanalyst, is *no.* In the first place, not everyone has the same right to the unconscious as a phenomenon of coded language. *In part, the unconscious is the ground where man buries both the other gender and the shadow of his own gender.* Why should he be given the right to the *pathos* of that shadowy land that Hegel

113

said was also a crime? Why, when the other gender has no right to
the same act in the economy of our culture? For centuries one part
of the world has, in Hegelian terms, been criminal toward the other,
in the sense of breaking or violating the ethical law of the other half
of the world. For centuries the race of men has taken possession of
ethical consciousness, claiming to have received the ultimate revelation, to have the power to legislate truth, all truth. For centuries,
the race of men has confused the human race with the *pathos* of their
own gender. In his *Phenomenology* Hegel clearly traces the way that
the spirit develops in our culture. Instead of acknowledging that
there are indeed *two* genders and that revelation may come from the
other gender—a revelation in itself and for itself—the race of men
claims a monopoly on truth and the exclusive right to legislate
everything: philosophy, law, politics, religion, science....

Thus all too often the consciousness of self bears the weight of
guilt as soon as it takes action. This happens whenever it claims to
determine all action and keeps the other gender in its shadow. This
happens whenever, denying its own ambivalence or involving the
other gender therein, it claims a monopoly on simplicity and right
because it has received a revelation of essence as essence is to itself.
In fact, of course, the manifestation of essence made to the male
consciousness is only the possibility of its return to self in a *pour-soi*.
The content of religious revelation, in fact, like the need to close that
revelation off, testifies to the need felt by *one* gender to afford itself
a god, a father god, a son god, a spirit god, and to insist that nothing
should be added to that revelation. Whereas women equate crime
with keeping, men, apparently, equate it with adding. She is not to
keep, he is to keep, without *any additions*. The obligation is always
the same, and the same in language: given that substance and the
first *topos* are female, the incarnate, manifest sign is masculine, and
nothing must go beyond it. This must all be closed and complete.
Perhaps so that the feminine cannot be added on? Does closure form
a part of the revelation of truth, *like* the intangibility of language?
Does this come down to the fact that the first mover and the first
matter, God and woman, cannot *touch*, according to one conception
of spirit formed by the race of men?

But the man-god, like the language of the male gender, is born of
woman, of an immaculate matter that has been celebrated as such,
even when it is clothed in various disguises. Between the two stands
man. Even as he is split between his darkness and his light, between
his night and radiance, she is torn apart, both by him and by his

114

world, between an *unmarked* primary matter on the one hand and the signs or emblems in which he cloaks her on the other. In theory she has never regained her wholeness, though this may occur in the future. Perhaps she knew it once, at the beginning of human time. This is the testimony of some cultures such as the tantric, which shows that everything is born *out of the lips* of one woman, or of some women. Hebrew culture, or at least the Kabbalah, shows the lips in the form of a double inverted *yod*, a double inverted tongue. As for Christianity, through the importance given to the sign of silence for the mother of Christ, it stresses the divine character of Mary's virginity and joining the lips takes on a religious meaning. Apart from silence, this is expressed by the sound *m:* the most perfect consonant, the darkest as well, the origin of all the others. In Indian culture, this *m* sound also designates that which has not become manifest, notably in the sacred syllable *ohm*.

Today we are faced with a comic collision of duty with duty that sometimes takes an institutional form. Few people worry about finding new ways to experience passion, or passions, about working out a new *pathos*, or rather a more ethical spirit, rooted in the world of the senses. On the other hand, the current raising of the stakes of duty has become pathetic, ridiculous, abstract. In fact, no one frames the issue in the context of a morality that somehow would include the *senses*.

If the female gender does make a demand, all too often it is based upon a claim for equal rights and this risks ending in the destruction of gender. Comedy arises out of this collision of rights and duties since it expresses the contradiction of an absolute in opposition. The tragicomedy we are witnessing recently functions perhaps as a kind of warfare since war belongs to the gender that has taken over the absolute as its own and since war is one of the symptoms showing us that the problem of the relation to the immediate has not been resolved. It is better to laugh than to indulge in murderous fanaticism! Yet the limit is hard to make out. We have to laugh while remaining vigilant, laugh to keep the worst at bay and keep our good health, laugh to ward off immediate acts of violence and to give ourselves breathing space. But any operation is an error if the self is equal to *one* and not to *two*, if it comes down to *sameness* and a split in sameness and ignores the other as other. According to this order the only innocent is one who remains without an operation: the stone, Hegel says, or the plant, perhaps. Women have often been deprived of their operations and become stones, plants. The women who make the man or assimilate into the male gender have no innocence, or have lost it. Such women are guilty in the eyes of *both* genders. But today the content of ethical action, *which is variable according to sex*, is disappearing. The universe that men have controlled does away with the contents of thought by destroying the world of the senses. A world that claims to be egalitarian—the same for all men and women—also destroys thought, by refusing to take account of the singular content (in some measure, the crime?) of any operation. Obviously, it is not one particular individual that is guilty, but a whole people and its claim on the *universal*. Whence the need to question the universal itself rather than setting up a comic war aimed at particular duties that don't even add up to the *sum* of the universal. It is one side's claim to lay down the law universally that is the error, the crime. It is not possible to divide up the stake of the booty, the rape, the contract. . . . For the shadow keeps on growing. One part of difference becomes ever more repressed, denied. One half of the truth no longer is opposed to the other in the context of the difference between genders. One part battles only with its ghosts, its shadows, its faults, its fears. . . . The insubstantiality of the enemy so exasperates it that it has to invent oppositions, incite them, intensify them, to the point of war. At this point action is so obviously destructive, a crime has so obviously been committed that calm returns since guilt has found an object to confront.

In fact, things are in some measure reversed: the individual is the formal moment of the operation in general, the *content* is constituted by laws and customs. The individual is born, and then seems to be born *a second time* of laws and customs. How these two births are embedded one in the other is a questions that no doubt often obscurely troubles anyone who considers man. Is this all a matter of genetics, nature? or of nurture and culture? This crucial question mandates a reconsideration of what Hegel tells us about the *double birth* of man and the way each of the two births is associated with one of the sexes. We need to raise the issue of what destiny, what duty is allocated to each gender. In fact, as long as the issue is not raised in these terms everyone washes his hands of the crime and the fault: *the universal is equivalent to the interest of the pour-soi.* If

116

no questioning of the universal occurs no modification of the individual and communal ethic is possible. Both are trapped in a destiny as if in a mold, a model, a borrowed ideal that prevents them from perceiving the truth and perceiving themselves as truth. No one is guilty. . . . The universal is guilty in that it imposes norms that kill or mortify life rather than realizing it fully in its forms. Between the natural universal and the universal of laws, customs, and truth there is no passage, no growth, no becoming.

The so-called natural destiny of the sexes is no longer natural. Laws and customs have already perverted nature in *the claim to the universal staked out by one side.* That man holds so strong a conviction that language is intangible, neuter, universal, is easy to explain: this conviction is set up as truth *by one side only.* And the theoretical prestige enjoyed by the *neuter* has its comic side. As well as a tragic side, which is associated with some violence. For everyone claims neutrality without noticing that he is talking about *one* neuter, *his* neuter, and not an absolute neutrality.

Today two neuters are presented to us as law: *the child*, especially dear to the disciples of Freud, and a *duty*, which supposedly comes down to us from the God of monotheism, especially when he is not incarnate. These enclaves of the neuter, which seek to be ethical, outside the war of the sexes, are, for as long as the tragedy of difference of the sexes and its fecundity remains unsolved, linked historically to the ascendancy and rule of technocracy, whether these be logocratic or the effects of the drives or the result of tools and machines. So, to take one example, to want the neuter in order to avoid a war waged with the most sophisticated techniques, is, to some extent, like staying with the same type of energy, a *one*, an irresponsible multiple, a quantitative, without stages or qualitative differences to ensure a change in energy. It is like retaining a *pathos* that has no just objectivity or subjectivity to offer the people as a whole, the peoples of the world, their generation, their regeneration, their growth.

But let us return to the child who is probably the hidden key to the polemic or apparent reconciliation surrounding the neuter. The child is a neuter noun only in some languages, Freud's, for example, or Hegel's. Thus it is very odd that international psychoanalysis, to name one of the arenas where this question comes up, is anxious to prop up its own neutrality through the notion of the neuter child.

This is achieved with the help of a bilingualism that goes unremarked and that in my opinion relates to the difference of the sexes as orthopedics relate to a hysterical aphasia or paralysis. For example, speaking in English was the way Anna O. in her talking cure would try to translate her feelings when she lacked words or representations in her native German. Even if the gender of the word *child* is sometimes neuter—just as the word *gender* is neuter in Greek, *to genos*, and it would be interesting to establish the relation between these two neuters in the passage of the *Phenomenology of Mind* I am rereading that concerns ethics in relation to the other—the child always has a sex. And it is, or would be, a great crime to wish the child to be neuter. In whose name is such a crime perpetrated? In God's name? The spirit's? Which one? As long as we live, we have a sex and are born of sexedness. So what death would we be imposing upon the child, the gender? on generation? on life? on sex? By what right, in what shadow, is the race of men, the language of men, authorized to envelop, bury, stifle the child as neuter? In the name of some neuter God that does not exist? Or in the name of an inability or refusal to share between the sexes?

There are two other ways the neuter enters *into* language, not just as content but as form(s). In my view one corresponds to *duty* and *law*. It would be something we inherited from Greco-Roman culture—a culture whose impact upon our indvidual and collective consciousnesses still deserves consideration. Law, rights, are said to be neuter or neutral but they have been laid down by one side only, and thus are in practice not neuter or neutral. This is shown in the content and form of the laws defining the substance of the adult individual. So this neuter has heavy repercussions and amounts to a solid bastion of resistance against any change in language and in the status of the subject. Even though the neuter or neutral offers remission from the wars and polemics among men, it offers no solution to the problem of the hierarchy of the male and female genders and its consequent injustices, no solution to the problem of the pathogenic neutralization—both individual and collective—of the languages and values that that hierarchy sets up. Let me add that in French at least the neuter is expressed by the same pronoun as the masculine: *"il* faut" and not *"elle* faut."

The realm of nature, which today has so powerful an influence over the mind even as we systematically destroy it, is also referred to in the neuter form: it's raining, snowing, hailing, etc. This has not always been the case. In our Greek antiquity, in our Eastern roots and ramifications, the universe is divided between the genders and they govern the elements together, though not always peacefully. Not only is the world of humans determined by the stars, as we say today, but the stars are also determined by men and by women—by *both* genders. In Greek tragedy, where certain basic elements of our social ethic are found, there is also talk of the loss of respect for the laws of nature and their representations in mythology. When they ceased to observe the differences between day and night, summer and winter, light and darkness, roots and flowers out of deference to social obligations that they had created in guilt, men lost micro- and macrocosmic governance, which can be exerted only with the *other* gender, not its shadowy remains or reverse, but with the *female gender*. The two genders between them share out micro- and macrocosmic governance. This destiny is neither neuter nor unique in its kind. All great cultures have said as much. Why are we forgetting it today? Which of our duties is more imperative, also more delightful, than to manage the order of the universe and of our flesh? Anything that carries us away from that duty or uproots us *into neuterness* annihilates the life in our bodies and in the body of the world, putting in their place empty and abstract mechanisms of feeling, of the content of thought, of art, of ethics.

If we still have a chance, it lies in *confronting the night of man's act with that part of woman that still lies in the night*. We don't have many other chances. And obviously it is not just a question of father and mother, of incest or the incest taboo, but of the existence of *two genders*, belonging to the same age, and of their different relation to life, to the senses, to form, to the divine, and to thought. This doesn't mean we should either void the question of the unconscious or double its constitution. The unconscious must be produced within the operation and not interpreted as permanence, immobility. Infinite repetition should be suppressed in the work. Once this occurs, otherness no longer belongs to *sameness* but reverts to the *other*. This is a limit, but this direction could lead us to a purity of the ethical sense.

Hegel talks about the purity of Antigone's crime. Perhaps there is an even greater purity: that of knowing why this so-called crime is forbidden, since it serves only the destiny that man makes for himself. To understand this would be to eliminate an apparent opposition and, for the female, to find the possibility of acting in affirmation. The female would then learn to be its own opposite and opposition within an ethical consciousness of its own. The female might lose hold on its *en-soi*, its essence. But it would no longer allow these to be defined by the other sex, the other gender. It would no longer constitute itself in opposition to a self-definition that forms a part of male effectiveness. The female gender, according to the order of its ethical duty, struggles with itself, between light and shadow, in order to become what it is individually and collectively. This growth, which is partly polemical, between consciousness and unconscious, immediacy and mediations, mother and women, has to remain open and infinite for and in the female gender. This growth is essential if the two genders are to meet. The greatest fault committed by the race of men was to deprive one gender of its ethical consciousness and of its effectiveness as a gender. That means that they separated effectiveness from substance. An American philosopher, Ty Grace Atkinson, if I understand her analysis, has called this move "metaphysical vampirism." I would add that the consequences amount to the same.

If women perform a duty that has been defined by the certainties of the other sex, their effectiveness necessarily remains contingent, except in a *pathos* of duty, which lacks any goal of its own, any ethical purpose. Women's purpose and its effectiveness, assuming the purpose is in fact theirs, is taken away: child and husband are taken away from women by society, the world of work by war. So women are amputated of the purpose of their action, forced to be disinterested, self-sacrificing, without ever having chosen or wanted this. The path of renunciation described by certain mystics is women's daily lot. But it is not possible to ask one people to be saintly in the name of a purpose espoused by another people. In fact—as Hegel understood very well—neither the people nor the gender are one. But one part lays claim to the right of ethical consciousness and leaves the other no purpose, no effectiveness, except as double, shadow, complement. *The human race has been divided into two functions, two tasks, not two genders.* Under pain of death, woman has renounced her gender. Man has done the same, though differently. Nonetheless his quarrel is with a god or a spirit made by his gender. I am often asked if man and woman will be able to communicate if two different genders are affirmed. Perhaps they will be commmunicating for the first time! In another way, since now they are closed up separately in figures of consciousness, of spirit, of race, which allow no passage between them.

Many of the most sophisticated minds of today conceive of sexual relations as a form of *incest,* whether conscious or unconscious. But this offers no answer to the problem of the human race and its partition. Incest is played out in terms of the generation gap and the *procreation* of gender, and does not refer to the *spirit* of gender. There is always a gap of age, of growth, of generation. It is perhaps in this sense that people talk about incest and its transgression as a way of overcoming cultural destiny. In fact, as I have noted in the case of the functioning of language, substance is first given by women, by mothers. This substance is then marked, branded by man, who cuts it up and uses it to make signs. But then man claims that these signs are, univocally, his truth. Equivocity, in its fashionable guise, does not necessarily represent war *in* the sign or the alloy. Antigone herself can be interpreted as an equivocal symbol, but she has already been drawn, withdrawn, toward one side alone.

The race of men lays a *second ground* underfoot, creates a meaning substance that supposedly knows no gender. This substance is almost tautologically opened up toward heaven, man's heaven, which he believes to be the source of his signs. And he forbids the other, the woman, to intervene, although he continues to venerate her as sacred and necessary for the return home. Man closes woman off from entering into the substance of language while asking her to keep being his own substance as speaking being. But she must remain dumb and unconscious of that truth. Man speaks with his fathers, with his brothers, he constructs a world while ordering the woman to keep up the house of life. All the same he claims that woman's task is to guard the dead. Woman fulfills man's needs as mother, matrix, body (both living and as a container-sepulchre), nurse. Apparently man wants woman only as mother and virgin, or sometimes, rather ambiguously, as sister—but not as woman, as other gender. Incest, from this point of view, does not solve the question of the relation between the genders. It remains in the generation of the living being or its denial, but never raises the issue of gender. Incest truly is blind—blind to gender! Oedipus is, I think, even blinder to the fact that he is dealing with a woman than with a mother. He knows nothing of sexual difference. The split of discourse and subject, which produces contradictions but no partners, clearly originates in the desire and the taboo of incest. No relation to the sensible world is established that could correspond to the effectiveness of a human race divided into two genders. Incest transgresses upon the ground of the double meaning, the bar of the *partial* meaning that is still and always ours. It does not eliminate the question, the obscure *polemos*, nor the potential fertileness of sexual difference. It plays a game with language and nature but always by splitting them, preventing them from uniting, from growing *simultaneously*. It plays the game of transgressing morphology in order to get the sap, some sap, rising again. This is no longer the sap of the subject that is a fruit fallen off the tree. Neither is it the roots. There is no present, actual way of presenting two subjectively sexed human beings.

Could it be this failure that has doomed man to technical being? Perhaps. Incapable of being generically, sexually alive, perhaps man has become a machine? Perhaps. Our era seems to indicate this. Perhaps we needed to go this far in order to understand that we must go back to the origins of the decline in our culture that began when one sex invaded the roots of the other like a parasite (that is both dependent and persecuted), when one sex loses its own roots and stands up erect as an immortal or spiritual being, failing to ensure its own growth as a mortal.

So we need to go back to the point at which the ethical fault was made and investigate the double uprooting that both men and women have suffered. At what point in their growth does it occur? The time is not the same for each. This explains how deceptive it is to look to incest as the solution or resolution of the question of gender. Woman, in fact, has remained between the material water and sky, the natural earth and sun, while man has become the worker who organizes the growth of the universe when he is faithful to his vocation as living being. But often man's rebellion and his power have taken the form of seizing control of matter in order to use it in the construction of his own world—or believing that this is possible—while renouncing his mortal becoming and the debt he owes to gender. Thus he has built a world that is both artificial and gimcrack, idealist and materialist, with no adequate articulation between these two poles, a world that claims to be neuter but that is man's alone, and which he would like to assimilate to all ground.

Recently there has been some suggestion that *androgyny* might be an ethical solution to the division of the genders. This is often intended as a generous solution. But I wonder how we are to identify with another gender if we have no definition of this gender as gender? Is it all just a question of imitating a role? a division of functions? or what? And what man today is ready to give up his power over society in order to know the social destiny that the female gender has experienced for generations?

In fact, is it possible for us *spiritually* to identify with the other gender, except in some idealist utopia, some new society where sex morphology is again suppressed by more or less delusional mental forms? Can this androgyny blaze a trail for an intergender ethics? If it exists, this trail must use sexual difference as both its setting out point and its destination, must take advantage of sexual difference on the road to spiritual discovery and affirmation.

If not, it represents a utopia of decadents plunged in their own world of fantasy and speculation, and producing an even weirder culture for the bodies that produce it. In my view, this is a case of one very small section of the community claiming to impose a new type of identity, of social style that indirectly still relies on fashion and commerce. Unless, again, this is one more leveling effect produced by the technocratic universe, promoting an energy of pseudo-neuteredness, neutrality, quantity, believing it is possible to do away once and for all with one gender, with the issue of gender, with genders. This is probably the most radical war we are faced with today, above all because it leaves us defenseless in our other wars.

THE UNIVERSAL AS MEDIATION

Zurich, March 25, 1986
Sixteenth Annual Hegel Conference at
the University of Zurich:
Moralität und Sittlichkeit

The family is the point where the two main branches of law converge—the law of estates and the law of social customs. But whereas the first kind of law has become hypertrophied and turned into the law of peoples, the other has atrophied and has either remained or become religious law. This means that the question of social and familial patrimony constitutes a large portion of civil and penal law and also, covertly, seems to determine the question of the ethical spirit, the *Sittlichkeit*.[1] The problem of nature conservation, of preserving life, and of our species as a living part of nature, seems no longer to concern civil organizations but has been tabled as a religious or private issue. The laws of social order are in fact directed toward problems of money and property growth for peoples and States.

We are beginning to see the limits of this conception of *Sittlichkeit*. We are beginning to grasp the idea that our species might disappear. Faced with this scenario, some men and women have decided to eat, drink, and be merry—and to hell with tomorrow. This kind of behavior is common during or before times of crisis when it seems foolish to work for the future. Other people grope toward making some necessary changes in the law, specifically in the rights enjoyed by the two genders[2]* and reproductive rights. But this evolution is a

1. In most cases, I have kept the German words *Moralität* and *Sittlichkeit*. In fact in French we have nothing that corresponds exactly to these terms. Sometimes I have used the usual Hegelian translations "morality and ethics," with the first referring more to the subjective, individual side, the awareness of something at once immediate, while the second refers to the objective side of morals and norms corresponding to the spirit of the community, the nation. In fact the way I use these terms is new since I refuse the opposition of immediate/mediate as it is developed in the Hegelian system.

2. Hegel and his translators consistently use the word *gender* but sometimes I have substituted *sex*. In fact the word *gender* is used to designate the difference of the sexes as well as grammatical gender. But gender in grammar expresses the reality of the two sexes in a very diverse and unequal way. If we are going to reconsider the question of culture and its systems of representation on the basis of sexualized bodies as places where different subjectivities are located we need to take issue with the economy of grammatical gender. Hence the necessity to separate the two notions of *gender* and *sex* in order to try to dialecticize a

grass roots affair, and there is no global consideration of issues that relate to natural law, civil law, and religious law. How all these different fields can intersect and interact is rarely given any thought. Hegel, however, did take on this gigantic speculative project. Thus, reviewing his ideas is a crucial task for us to undertake today.

Hegel analyses how the law wavers between two poles:

—the prevalence of a formalism that is largely arbitrary, needed to mark a decision or to set boundaries, yet always in search of some solid content to fill the forms out.

—the existence of some laws that stand close to the content of action and that show little variation in their expression: thou shalt not kill, steal, etc.

The first of these two kinds of laws is often defined or redefined by the society or the State, whereas the second still derives from a morality or an ethics that, at least originally, is of divine order.

We are far from solving the problem of reconciling the laws of god(s) and the rules emanating from human governance. The latter are constantly multiplying yet are forever inadequate in number. They are too formal, inadequate to meet each individual situation. Divine law, therefore, takes up the slack. It alone is operational in certain contexts: sexuality, love, and marriage, at least in part. Historically, divine law is of female origin.

Since Marx, since Freud, we have been habitually forced to face the question of a law that could be applied to lovers or married couples and the way they are located at the junction of private and public, of subjective and objective, of *Moralität* and *Sittlichkeit*.

But there is still much resistance to this movement, particularly because our discourse is incapable of rethinking a universal as mediation and not as truth resulting from arbitrary forms. There is resistance on the part of cultural law as it manifests itself in civil laws and holy commandments.

---

point that Hegel never differentiated. Thus, the word *sex* is used in regard to male and female persons and not just to male and female genital organs.

* Traditionally, the region mapped by the English words *gender* and *sex* does not correspond to that of the French words *genre* and *sexe*. Most notoriously, *le sexe*, which in modern usage has come to mean "the sexual organs" as well as "sex," is a common colloquial word for penis. The inapplicability of the singular noun *le sexe*, with its highly phallic connotations, has been one of Irigaray's most crucial points as a feminist theorist. Hence her need to footnote a change in her use of the words *le sexe* and *le genre*, a change that in fact moves French closer to English usage.—Tr.

We still lack a point of intersection between the two, just as we lack a culture of union for the couple, and a culture of sexuality and of love. This lack is the result of the separation between the genders and of the fact that they have not entered the historical stage at the same time.

Our societies began as gynocracies. Primary to our cultures is a female religious power linked to the cult of Aphrodite. This power is shared between mothers and daughters. At this stage group organization is a form of priesthood. But the religious is indivisible from the civil. The task of the ministers of Aphrodite is to tend human order as it relates to natural growth and love. Reproduction of the species is often ensured outside matrimony. This Aphroditian order is replaced by the Demeterian order: the power (*puissance*) of *the mother within* marriage.

During these two eras of gynocratic rule, relations between mothers and daughters are both naturally and divinely important. In the rule of Aphrodite the earth's fruitfulness remains spontaneous, linked to water, dampness, valued for its flowering. Under the rule of Demeter the earth's fruitfulness is the result of agriculture, and it is associated with the solar seasons that determine the harvest.

These two periods in the power of women, periods dominated by the importance given to the earth's fertile creation of flowers and fruits, yield to patriarchy, to the inauguration of patrimony and its masculine name, the corresponding need for civil law, the institution of all the various forms of the State, and the beginning of wars between peoples.

Today both the couple and marriage still bear traces of these different eras. Over the world they are divided up, with women being associated with a respect for nature, places, holy things, and peace, and men being associated with the business of acquiring and keeping property (even if this means a few wars, a few sacrifices),[3] of establishing the social order, organizing and defending the State, etc.

Little thought has been given to the fact that the human couple simultaneously joins together the gynocratic and the patriarchal

---

3. There are two meanings of the word *nature*. Patriarchal cultures, especially of late, often interpret the meaning of *nature* in accordance with a *human nature* that they have themselves defined. Yet in the first instance nature means earth, water, fire, wind, plants, living bodies, which precede any definition or fabrication that tear them away from roots and origins that exist independently of man's transforming activity.

129

eras. Hence the lack of any law that is sexed positively, hence the imbalance for the couple and between the couple and society.

☆

The issue of the universal as mediation has to be reformulated in terms of the problem of the law for the couple, as well as the investigation of the institution of marriage as a unit in which the rights of each partner are ill defined. According to Hegel, within the family, there is no longer an individual for self *(pour soi)*. The family is determined by its *felt* unity, by love, by the consciousness of having an individuality that is essence in self and for self. But the family is not a covenant, except at the time of the wedding, and perhaps not even then. . . . The family is a *substantial* unit in which the individual units that make up the *number* fuse and also thereby lose their individual rights. The family stands between a rather ill-defined substantial unit and a distinct part of the functioning of the State, of civil society. Within this definition of the family, there is a certain aporia. The *for self* lacks determinants, laws, rights. Family members, Hegel says, keep the right to life. But how is this exercised? If the family is defined as a substantial unit giving rise to the *en-soi* and the *pour-soi* of each person *as well as* a legal unit that limits its existence and expansion, each person thereby has a common share in physical and spiritual property that has been *poorly defined* by both male and female parties. In fact, he or she is responsible to civil society for a suit that has no legal status and that therefore remains *limitless*. According to Hegel this jurisdiction comes into force for the individual only when the family breaks up.

Within the family each person *only has the right to life*. But what is life? What is respect for life if each person has no responsibility within the undifferentiatedness of the familial *substance?* Within this whole in which each person is merely a stage how can there be an ethics of the physical and spiritual life of each person, male and female?

Obviously, there is the authority of the father and the mother, a very asymmetrical authority, as it turns out. The father gives or takes the name, the property, the rights to the spiritual, particularly in the area where family and society, nature and culture, meet. The mother is guardian of the substance in that she is the reproductive and nourishing body. She risks taking over the place of the earth as the family moves away from agriculture in particular and from respect for nature in general. This stage coincides with that in which the gods are lost to her. The female gods, *in so far as they are linked to the family*, are gods, or rather goddesses, of fertility. The loss of these gods or goddesses coincides with the separation between *mother and daughter*, the daughter's abduction by the god of the dead and the underworld, and their *marriage*.

Ever since this time, the daughter has been exiled from her land in order to become a wife, and the wife becomes a mother in the genealogy of her husband. This duty of hers, this right of his, cuts woman off from her roots and reroots her in the family of her husband, where she must provide the substance. She provides earth to the name of her husband and his ancestors within the monogamous patriarchal order.

The woman must leave her mother in order to become a mother. This is a matter to be decided among men, originally among gods, and the mother has no right to protect or defend her daughter in the transaction. According to our mythological tradition, the only right established to oppose this separation of mother and daughter is the right to bring *sterility to the earth*. Perhaps we need to interpret the current squandering of fruits and harvests, the exploitation and destruction of the earth as one effect of this break in the genealogical line of women that Freud, for example, declares to be necessary and that is a manifestly real phenomenon in any number of economico-political regimes.

The exclusive emphasis on the woman's role as mother has gone in step with a lack or respect for the natural order. The *cult* of maternity is often *opposed* to the respect for natural fruitfulness, though this deep and secret contradiction is always being denied. But the cult, when it makes an appearance as such, is the cult of the *son's mother*. The love of cosmic fertility is linked to the relation between mother and daughter. Anything that works to promote natural fruitfulness is to be found between Demeter and Kore, for example. If Kore is taken away from her mother by the god of the dead, if she is—like a certain number of her sisters in mythology—covered over with earth, buried or closed up in the rocks, her mother and the whole of the earth become sterile. Demeter cannot create in the absence of her daughter, Kore knows happiness only in the presence of her mother. Mother and daughter must be able to see and feel one another if the earth is to be fruitful, if the weather is to favor the crops.

The mother-daughter couple is also divine. In the era of gynocracy nature and the gods are not separate. The sacrifice of the (female) one to the others (or to the Other) marks the passage to another era in which natural life is subordinated to spiritual becoming. No thought is given as to which nature and which spirit are involved here, especially in the right to life, the so-called inalienable right of every individual.

Women are indoctrinated to believe that their *duty* is to preserve life for the other, particularly the child, not for themselves. In past times, and sometimes even today, the woman has to be sacrificed to the child, in childbirth, for example, but more generally in the obligation laid upon her to bear children. The choice of child over mother can be understood as a mandatory sacrifice to the husband's genealogy. No right protects the woman's life against violence in the home, against unwanted pregnancies. A right that should be guaranteed and protected by society and the State is instead a barely tolerated claim, sometimes partially heeded but always at the mercy of decisions made by specific individuals: this doctor, this judge, this expert will consult their consciences and decide on a woman's right, within a context that allows no generalizations. The process has to be started from scratch and pursued in isolation by each woman in turn since there is no legal recourse that is specific to woman.

Yet this is a question of right to life. But life can only be thought about, guaranteed, protected if we give consideration to *gender* as one constituent of the human race, not only in reproduction but also in culture, spirit.

Between the morality of an individual who has been locked away within the family, on the one hand, and the *Sittlichkeit* of a whole people, on the other, we need to establish an ethics *of the couple*, a place, a bond, where the two halves of the natural and spiritual world can be and change. Every moral inertia, every imprisonment within a good conscience, ought to find its limits in the irreducibility of sexual difference, in the unceasing interrogation between the two genders, in a polemic for the right to natural and spiritual life for both men and women.

Like every living being I am searching for an idea of the State, but what I find is the problem of the family, and within the family, the undifferentiated state of the couple. This problem is interfamiliar as well intrafamilial. In order to differentiate between individuals it is not even possible to invoke the gods of the ancestors on the two sides, for they are not necessarily available. They are not equally respected: the wife no longer honors the name or the property of her father and her mother, at least in public. Could this be one reason why she is hidden away in the home?

The gods of the couple, in fact, are not necessarily incarnate in the ancestors. We lack a notion of a finite or a *concrete* infinite that would permit an infinite becoming within the finite. Ancestors testify to a genealogy, a history, not an infinite. Perhaps this succeeds in conferring on history the idea or the illusion of a *historical* infinite. In history the dissymmetry between the ancestors tends to result in the division of history into periods, rather than in its continuous growth and development.

The spirit as *history* and not as spiritualization of nature can be interpreted as the effect of a *double nature* of the spirit instead of its entry into matter. History is the soil in which a second nature, a double nature grows: cultural, spiritual nature, which goes beyond its natural potential. Do heads roll in every period for this reason? The finiteness that tries to outdo itself in different ways in different periods seems linked to a process of *forgetting the culture of gender,* of sex, which, as the war of the generations reminds us, is necessary. The periods of history signify a split with nature. This split makes itself felt as an opposition between moment and eternity, as the organization of another time scheme, a double time scheme. Lacking therein is continuity, the articulation between vegetative growth and social clock time. As soon as this passage from one to other is erased in favor of an opposition between one and other, we find a sacrifice and an exclusion of women. The spirit cuts its roots and settles in the ashes of a burned offering—plant, animal, human— that women are not allowed to witness. This exclusion seems to serve to redouble the sacrifice.

The *en-soi* of the race as a whole is, thus, heterogeneous to, other than, the life of individuals, and their growth. But this otherness is not based in a limitation of respective desires. It is inaugurated by a sacrifice, a tragedy, an exclusion, and by the opening of another space-time than that of nature. Within the family, then the race, then the nation, something is hidden that allows the articulation of spirit, of time, of history. This something is the maternal-female that invisibly continues its work of underpinning the existence of the whole social body.

To set something aside or hide it in this way is an ethical offense. It corresponds in large measure to the fact that women are sacrificed to war and fellowship among men. On the other hand, it serves to keep women out of social governance and divided among themselves. This offense against women will be systematically revealed and repeated through the designation and sacrifice of a scapegoat that belongs to the social body in a more visible way than women do. Periodically throughout history, men will designate a guilty person or persons, and will wage war on them. Beneath this cyclical time scheme lurks the offense that has already been committed against the other gender.

From the time that this social order cuts itself off from nature, the individual is masked as social entity. The resulting loss of identity makes its mark on ancient tragedy. Henceforward, men—kings, heroes, people—will be travestied and at the mercy of fate. This fate is both tempered and passed on in Greek, and later in Roman, legal proceedings. The twin duties—to wear a mask and to submit to necessity or to the law—follow upon the separation of man from life. This drama is played out in the appropriation of woman's sex by man in the rape of Kore by the god of the underworld, the abduction and sacrifice of Iphigenia during the Trojan war, the legalized murder of Clytemnestra, the burial of the Furies beneath the city of Athens, the glory of Athena who proclaims herself daughter of the father alone and denies her maternal heritage, the incarceration of Antigone in the stone cave outside the city.

This plot is often interpreted today, particularly in psychoanalysis, as the result or the threat of incest. But when incest occurs it is already the outcome of a blindness, a loss of limits for man as man when he erases woman's genealogy and the relations of mothers and daughters and exploits them in the interests of male filiation and fellowship among men. Whence the nostalgia, the wish to regress, that men feel toward their mothers, their births. The incest committed by Oedipus is the now unconscious crime of erasing gender identity, which sends the son back to his mother as if she were the only possible female place. The offense of Oedipus, of psychoanalysis, is to forget the importance of the mother-daughter relation, and of women's genealogy, especially in their relations to natural fruitfulness but also in their necessary part in constituting a living and ethical gender identity.

The confusion between the ideal and historical reality for which Hegel has sometimes been reproached is possible thanks to his incorrect analysis of the living community. There is an a priori and an a posteriori that have not been analyzed: the ethical totality corresponds to a race of men who rely upon a law drafted and administered by men.

That absolute spirit and its expression do not coincide can be partially explained in terms of a faulty or inadequate analysis of the race as a unit. The historic positivity of the State, for example, is still the corpse or the remains of a society whose uniqueness of spirit has been poorly analyzed. Hegel has an aesthetic conception of society and the State that masks many horrors.

What is a race/people? How can it be defined if no thought has yet been given to sexual difference? The race of men forgets that it is a race by function of its gender. It gives thought to many things but not to its gender as the bond that unites its members. Does the race of men not think of itself as a race? As the *substance* of a race? Does this result from the status of the couple and of marriage?

In marriage there are two kinds of *for us*. Now, these two *for uses* seem to make up an undifferentiated substance within the family. This means that the family sacrifices at least *one* and maybe *two* of the *for uses*. For what? For a unity that is neither pure immediacy nor pure mediation. The family is linked to natural immediacy if only because it *belongs to gender* and because it *reproduces*. There is little stress on belonging to gender as a difference inscribed in nature itself. That natural immediacy is almost always sexualized is a fact never considered to be one stage in spiritual sublation. That natural immediacy should have a sex is considered only in the context of reproduction and is never developed into a spirituality of the body, the flesh. Thus the natural immediacy of the couple is not spiritualized. Kinship is supposedly spiritualized. But this spirituality often conceals the sacrifice of nature and spirit, even though it is represented as their spiritual union. In this sense, ancestors figure as gods of the hearth. But ancestors are always multiple, bilateral, unequal in their rights, and they can serve to make the couple divine only if they are spiritualized within their *genders*. Otherwise, they turn into repressive systems conducted against the spiritualization

135

of gender and into all that makes us fall back into the natural immediacy of birth, reproduction, decay.

So ancestors serve a family unit that necessarily strikes us as the death of the individual. For centuries, this death has been more obvious on one side of sexual difference than on the other. Woman must leave her family, her home, her name, to take those of her husband. Even the child of her flesh will bear the name of her husband's genealogy. Abducted from her ancestors, particularly her mother, she is consigned to the natural immediacy of reproduction. Motherhood, in turn, is valued only if it is the bearing of *sons*, not daughters. Thus the family falls back in various ways into nonspiritualized nature: the woman insofar as she is torn away from her own culture and reduced to the flesh of man ("flesh of his flesh") and to reproduction, man insofar as he has failed to spiritualize his sex, and is split between his membership in the family unit and his work to build the race—while all the while remaining, secretly, the son of his wife. Man's relation to his mother remains unresolved. Irresolute, does he *confuse species and gender? Does he collapse gender into species?* Man remains a child, part of human nature, insofar as he does not think through his relation to his gender. As a son who may have to measure up to his brother by sacrificing his sister, he also submits to natural immediacy in his maternal genealogy. Thus, in effect, his relation to the family is both undifferentiated and divided in that he must be a *son* and a *citizen* at the same time. This *at the same time* does not make for a continuity as Hegel would have it. The spirit of the races will never undergo sublation in the relation of the citizens to birth, motherhood, to their own gender, to their growth. Citizens as a gender are cut off from their roots in the body, even as they remain bound, as bodies, to their mother-nature. Unable to resolve this issue, they let it determine their relations with women, whom they restrict to the role of mothers. Such tyranny is the symptom of a *hidden* immediacy and of revenge. Both of these are the trace of a natural *pathos* that has not been spiritualized. This pathos reduces the life of man and race to a *fate*. But this fate is the effect of an unconscious decision on man's part. He wants to be only and wholly a citizen. The spirit of the race has for centuries in fact been the spirit of the race of men, who are sustained by the women who serve them as mothers, nurses, caretakers, providers of flesh. Woman, on the other hand, must submit to a fate decreed by her father, her brothers, her husband, her "king," and by civil law as conceived by the race of men, the State. As a woman, she must remain invisible in society, keep faith with her immediate, natural fate as reproducer of the body, or bodies, a fate she can fulfill but that, as an obligation, does not constitute a spiritualization of her nature. Obviously, she can transform this fate into spiritual duty, but this does not mean that she has thereby spiritualized her body as the female side of the covenant within the couple. She has perpetuated a natural state without transforming it and without modifying the spirit of the race on the basis of its most elemental productive and reproductive cell: the family, the couple, that place where the regenerative and procreative union of and between the genders occurs.

This absence of any dialogue within the couple, this failure of sexual dialectic (on condition of rethinking the sense of the method), perverts the spirit of the individual, of the family, of the race. The concrete, which Hegel seeks in the individual, has its sexual dimension cut away. The individual is already *abstract*. This abstractness forces us to think of the family as an undifferentiated substance and not as the place of individuation, of a spiritual differentiation that can occur only if there is some polemic between the sexes.

The suppression of this miniwar between living beings operates by reducing women as women to silence, by equating women as mothers with nature, and by obliging them to sit on their hands rather than act as citizens with an active, open, and responsible role to play in building the city. The passage to the race has been perverted, falsified, in its relation to life.

If the spiritual characteristics of a people are rooted in national geography, on the world level a national spirit also translates the fact that it belongs to two genders. But the decoding and expression of this relation to life and to nature is often paralyzed, veiled, concealed. Regional, national traits *mask* the gender trait. Could this be because it marks the place of the *universal trait?* But it is *two*. No thought is given to that. Our age forces us to come back to this issue, for reasons such as our immediate or mediatized knowledge of peoples, nations, regions. These in fact risk losing their special characteristics because of the importance of industry and commerce, and, on a different level, because they place themselves as diverse units within a single discourse, a single logic, a race of men that does not think of itself as possessing a sex. The mystery we had thought to discover in distant lands turns out to be very familiar, very near to our hearts: the mystery of gender, of ourselves insofar as we are two genders. Did this nearness exist in the time of the cult of Aphrodite?

Contemporary science has its own way of showing us this path that leads back to ourselves. Biology teaches or reminds us that some of our chromosomes are sexed. Psychoanalysis stresses that we cannot forget the influence sex wields over our whole lives. All the sciences give us the same information: sociology, ethnology, economics, etc. The resistance of certain hard sciences amounts to a delay in comprehension that reveals itself in the way the latest particles to be discovered have been given women's names, and called "charmed"—that is to say the terms of a love affair are transposed into the most technically sophisticated research. This still has to be understood and interpreted.

The most powerful goal of interpretation is the analysis of discourse as sexualized and not neuter. This can be demonstrated with linguistic and semiotic tools. To undertake this task is to complete that extra turn into self-consciousness that Hegel failed to make: reflexion upon discourse itself as a content that is the outcome of its forms, forms that are arbitrary. This task in no way implies the destruction of Hegel's philosophy since he points out the method. But this philosopher of the universal, of the achieved whole, of the absolute spirit, happily has his limits, as do we all. He was a male, he lived between the eighteenth and nineteenth centuries, he was mortal. I might add that he was shaped by his language and that language's way of expressing gender. Of course, other character traits were also determinants of Hegel's character. However, those I have mentioned seem to me the most important from the point of view of the universal.

How would Hegel have reacted to these scientific statements? Would he have turned over the becoming of history as far as it relates to the ultimate interrogation of language as not neuter but sexualized? Would he have questioned the logic of the discourse he relied upon, realized the limits of the mediating role of language and the need to rethink and transform language as vehicle of mediation? His rejection of a priori statements, his respect for life and nature, must surely have urged him to lead the dialectic on to consider these questions. Why did he fail to suspect their importance? Is it a question of his times? Of silence about sexuality? Of belief in the watertight barrier separating public and private domains, the gods of the hearth and the gods of the city? A wish to suppress the gods? A confusion between the modesty and the barbarousness of the spirituality of the sexual, of gender, of the family? This thinking, this culture, demand a change in discourse. All the resistance to considering these issues takes place on the inside of a logic that does not acknowledge its own limits.

Hegel's method is based on contradiction, on contradictory propositions. Yet sex does not obey the logic of contradiction. It bends and folds to accomodate that logic but it does not conform. Forced to follow that logic, it is drawn into a mimetic game that moves faraway from life. The woman who acts the man (or the woman . . .), the man who acts the woman (or the man . . .), the wife who acts the mother, the man who acts the father, are not spiritualizing their nature. They submit to a social logic unsuited to their nature. They have, within them, a duality that would already allow them to apply a new method. Each man or woman is physiologically his or her sex and the production of that sex. Each man or woman is his or her gender and is potentially a father or a mother. This articulation of the two within him or within her is not *contradictory* but requires a method in which *the one is not reduced to the other.* Gender, rather than, as is claimed, maternity or paternity, has infinite and absolute charge, and power (*puissance*). Children kill their parents, Hegel asserts. Genealogy takes shape as the line of infinity but it is a sectile, fragmented infinity: one + one + one . . . that postulates one people, one idea, one God as meeting point. This (masculine) one + one + one . . . is often in secret projected synchronically into the possession of the one + one + one . . . women (or more rarely men) and into the illusion that this addition is capable of solving the question of the infinite. But gender does not work this way. This multiple as delusive resolution of the absolute probably corresponds to the abolition of sexed gods, and the absence of any spiritualization of gender.

The process whereby gender might become perfect is lacking in Hegel, and indeed in ourselves. If gender were to develop individually, collectively, and historically, it could mark *the place where spirit entered human nature,* the point in time when the infinite passed into the finite, given that each individual of a gender is finite and potentially infinite in his or her relation to gender.

Hegel investigates any postulated unit with great vigilance. Yet, in his view, the family constitutes a unit. It has to, since there is no dialectic between the sexes. This imposed unit upsets the whole of Hegel's construction. This is where spirit fails to penetrate into nature to spiritualize it. Obviously, every home cannot begin the complete adventure of the spirit from scratch. It must continue the adventure. For this becoming to be possible, there must be some representation in law of the rights of each sex as different parties. The gods must be kept, they must be inscribed in law as visible representations of concrete living realities. As ethical and responsible, as full participants in the order of the family and therefore of the people, women must become socially visible in their sexed singleness. *Otherwise the social body splits off from the natural body* (civil law from natural law). Hegel always bet on the continuity between living nature and the spirit in his debates with pure empiricists and idealists. But he omits one link in the chain of life, in life's passage to spirit within the couple, the family. In the bosom of the family, man drowns in an ocean of primitive undifferentiation. He can regain his individuality only when he leaves the family. This means that the living development of individuals in the family is interrupted, split. The evolution of individuals is split off from their nature because they betray their gender. Hegel is doomed to do what he wished not to do, because of a paralysis of will between the genders in the family. *He gives no thought to the living being as a sexed being.* This failure in Hegel's thought, though not entailing the a priorism of Kant or Fichte, maintains a break in the spiritualization of the living and of nature. This break is reflected in the society and the State. It is also expressed, as an unavowed repression, in the claim that there is a *neuter* universal.

To keep faith with life the universal must manifest and maintain the becoming of living things as they are: *sexed.* When it fails to keep faith with this concrete micro- and macrocosmic reality, the universal is an abstract obligation to feel that lacks any method to think through that abstraction.

If we are to go beyond this separation we need to think about gender. Will this be dialectical thinking? In one sense, yes, in another, no. As the genders are neither opposed nor in contradiction. One result of a method of the universal that pays no attention to gender is that the genders are imagined as being in conflict. Gender difference mandates a new thought, a new discourse, that would solder together the division between the gods and the law. The tutelary gods of the hearth must be represented in civil law and the State, or the family will be destroyed—as is probably happening today. But these household gods must be sexually differentiated if we are to ensure the defense of the life of individuals bound by matrimony or simply living together as couples. Such gods, as I see it, do not make up the two sides of a single god, but are two divinities who can give birth to the divine. God cannot be god and be unjust. In order to avoid such injustice, god must be divine for both genders while protecting and facilitating the development of their lives. The god (or gods) must also promote the energy of the couple and of the family as a transition between the individual and the State, rather than a place where a split occurs that impedes the passage of nature into spirit. For in that case there is no longer that realization of the concrete universal that Hegel sought. There is no *mediation* between the sexes as concrete matter, substance of the family, and then of society. The substance Hegel talks of is a *relationship*. Should law begin and end in that relationship, moving from the particular to half of the universal? In this way law would remain what it is meant to be: an ethical relation among individuals rather than the imposition of abstract forms in order to put an end to something unreal or conditional.

This constitution of ethical relationships among individuals usually goes unconsidered, undifferentiated. In this sense only religion pays any real attention to familial *duties*. As opposed to familial rights all the time! But since religion has been represented as male monotheism for centuries, the rights of women not only to life but also to sexual pleasure are given little specification by religious thinkers. The right of gender is forgotten or sacrificed to the right of money, of property as it passes through the male line, to the right of the state. Despite the message of the New Testament (which is clearly a complex one as far as the absent heavenly father is concerned), Christianity makes a one-way demand that women give up their family rights and their female genealogy in favor of the right of the father, of his wealth, his genealogy. The New Testament hints at quite a different method and path. But who has understood, for example, the ways in which Christ is bound to his mother's genealogy? Who preaches that we should emulate Christ's politically militant relation with women? The force of patriarchal rights, already felt at the time of Christ, continues to distort his words and his actions and to propose a sacrificial purpose that is quite at odds with Christ's message.

The only possible way of reconciling objective spirit and absolute spirit seems to be to rethink the notion of gender, of the genders, and of their ethical relationships. This will modify the data in presence. Objective spirit will no longer be made up of the head and the trunk, the spirit and the body that are bonded together so poorly that growth depends upon periodic wars, suppressions, destructions, and sublations—assuming that any bonding has in fact occurred in History; the record of the latest philosophers rather indicates the contrary. Hegel also insists on the fact that the spirit had never really entered into History, thus concurring with the pessimistic view Freud and others have held about civilization. The nonreconciliation of absolute spirit and objctive spirit can be interpreted on the basis of the unresolved split of body/spirit, sex/body that haunts gender and the genders.

But the spirit that is alien to gender is abstract. This abstractness and the loss of that concrete, sensual immediacy that was always Hegel's point of departure block the passage from subjective into objective, from objective into subjective. Hegel sought to keep faith with nature but to do this one must pass through that question of sex and the spirit. The increase in so-called objective cultural effects produced by an inadequate dialectic of subjective and objective risks burying us under its spiritless shell, overwhelming us with its pestilential waste products.

A kind of pseudo-objectivity claims to lay down the law today. It lays claim to a whole range of rights without protecting that most elementary right: the right to life. Thus the laws on private property that place no limits on the deleterious effects of a consumer society are nothing more than an abstract idea guaranteed by civil society, by money, by ideology, but lack any roots in space and time. Our contemporary civil society seems, in fact, incapable of managing what it has set in place economically. We seem to lack the energy and the ideas needed to cultivate our economic resources while respecting life and liberty. The State, which, according to Hegel, must rule over civil society, is unable to take on this role for economic reasons. Therefore it yields to the demands of civil society. Its major concern is not the universal but money. But what is money without the search for mediations that promote life and the spiritualization of human beings?

What do the really rich do today? They buy a piece of land or a woman that shows no trace of the pollution produced by their wealth. In order to acquire this piece of nature, where it is still possible to have a life, they force others to suffer conditions that deprive them of the right to life and thought. The State is incapable of preventing the rich from doing this because it is dependent upon wealth. In fact, the State does the same thing. Aiding and abetting capital, the State shrugs off its inability to manage the universal by affecting the *cosmopolitan.* This is nothing but a potpourri of the special traits of different peoples and usually entails a loss of geographical roots. The human race can no longer live, or live with itself, this way. It thereby abandons or neglects its right to life. There is one chance left for the human race to stop this process of dispersion and destructuring: to think and practice a *sexualized* ethic, rights for gender and the genders that have been virtually unknown outside the reproductive duties of the family cell and the refusals to obey a law that has no validity between the sexes. To seek freedom of relations between same-sex partners and the legalization of pornography no doubt constitutes a departure from traditional heterosexual duty, particularly the duty to reproduce. There is still no question of achieving a sexualized ethics. Does transgression of an existing morality perhaps indicate an expectation of better times? As the homosexual passage often is in every life and at each stage in a life?

☆

Hegel says that wars are necessary. They cut off heads and regimes just as one cuts the corn. Later, the harvests grow again, Hegel writes. Wars are one of the serious parts of life, and make us all hold our tongues. Hegel talks about war the way some people talk about nature. He makes it into a person and lends it a power that goes beyond all reason, whether magic or divine.

Nature had its gods and they were sexualized. Who are the gods of History? What is this historic destiny Hegel talks about? Does it run parallel with the anatomic destiny attributed to woman? For the Greeks, *ananke* started to play a part after the sexualized gods who ruled nature were suppressed. *Ananke* sems to be the place we can still find the natural laws that were forgotten even in their divine significance. The peoples and womankind would obey natural laws that have never been thought about as such or spiritualized. Destiny weighs upon them. The masses would be the masked vehicle of this destiny. Among other things, the masses would express the private violence performed against gender, particularly the female gender.

Hegel holds Christianity responsible for the destiny of History, in particular for the failure of spirit in the people. "Render unto Caesar the things that are Caesar's, and unto God the things that are God's" is a dictum, for example, that would account for contemporary individualism. This analysis seems wrong to me. The separation of the

State and the divine has been inscribed in the status of gender in the family and in the culture at least since the Greeks. Well before Christ, Aeschylus and Sophocles describe one stage in that division, the fall of the sexed gods and the inauguration of a social power that is not divine.

Hegel puts too much responsibility upon Christianity. Christianity is both less and more than he thinks. It is different. The incarnation corresponds to the attribution of limits and not to that infinite individuality that Hegel talks about. The split between Christian innerness and Roman outerness is rather a caricature of a real situation that had existed since the family genealogy of the household gods had been sacrificed to war and to fellowship among men. There can be no absolute innerness and no absolute knowledge of the individual until the divine has been *made flesh*, especially by means of a couple.

But the nonhierarchical difference of the sexes already makes such absolutes impossible, since the one endlessly limits the freedom of the other. If gender is respected, there can be no absolute freedom, since the genders limit themselves and each other mutually, both as genders and in production-reproduction. Does this imply a potential unity between inside and outside? This is a difficult question. It always obeys a given time frame that is much more rapid than the notion of period or era. It also gives a much larger place to *perception*. For a dialectic of the couple to occur, we need an art of perception that cannot be reduced either to a pure innerness or a pure outerness but passes ceaselessly from one to the other. This art requires that concrete perception be detailed and attentive, a perception that as autoaffection is individual, is copulative as the privileged space of heteroaffection, and finally is collective. This training in perception requires a time frame that passes not through destruction or sublation but through heeding and knowing a culture of the senses as such. Finally we achieve access to progressive levels of intensity and to a contemplation of nature in itself, of itself and of the other, which philosophy has disregarded as a stage in spiritual development and fulfillment.

This art of perception is indispensable for the ethical becoming of the couple, of the family (in the widest meaning of that word), yet is lacking in our culture. Even the fine arts pay little heed to it. The East, India in particular, and ancient Greece, are examples of cultures who cultivated this art. Hegel, and most of our contemporary thinkers, spend little time on these cultures. What is more, when art does show an awareness of the flesh this does not mean that the ethics of the couple has been resolved. It gives the nod to the importance of the issue and to its valuable aesthetic potential. Nonetheless there is a danger that ethics should become a part of aesthetics and seen as secondary to the life of the people, pleasant but not essential to spiritual development. This avoids the need to go beyond contradictions and oppositions and achieve a truly sexualized thought. Above and beyond all dichotomies thought must transform the *pathos* of human energy into respect for the life of the self, of the other, of others, in the context of spiritualizing and divinizing gender and the genders. Without this concern the right to property becomes or becomes once more a right without content.

Today, the abstract character of the right to property can be seen in all the bodily damage we suffer even as we cower behind the walls of our private enclaves. Environmental noise, air pollution, the violent irruption of the media and telecommunications into our homes, the consequent necessity to take drugs and undergo surgery are just a few of the signs that life—that inalienable right according to Hegel—is not being respected.

One essential if we are to achieve a universal ethic is respect for the perceptions of every man and woman as conditions of physical and spiritual life. If we lose the use of our senses, we die. But the senses also serve to mediate thought. Without the senses, thought is impossible, it becomes pure automatism, heedless of liberty or of intention.

The senses are linked to that elementary function of social living: *sex*. This is not merely a question of reproduction, of intercourse in the service of generation, but is one of the fundamental modes of our human condition.

Our senses stand at the juncture between the individual and the social, the private and the public. The right to the senses is a private and public right, individual, familial, natural, and civil. Our governments don't care much about hunger in the world, but they care even less about respect for our bodies as the meeting ground of the private and the public. Not much thought is given to ways in which the subjective as body and flesh might be experienced as the objective. A subjectivity that knows nothing of itself as object cannot really be a subjectivity. What subjectivity has no knowledge of itself as science of the body? of the flesh? of gender? What kind of *pathos* is at work here? Why does it need to go in search of its moderation in God, but in a God of its own gender?

A feeling that lacks knowledge of gender as a dimension in attraction, in love, in spirit, in ethics—what does such a feeling correspond to? To an intentionality that has no object? To an instinct? But how is an instinct to receive ethical training? A drive? Respect for gender seems to be the only dimension that puts an end to destruction, appropriation, infinite dispersion, etc.

In our times, multiplicity confounds all our efforts to bring things together, and disintegrates subjective and objective. It also destroys the time frame to the extent in which that establishes a perspective on the *this here*. Whereas our time frame demands an acceleration to match the mobility of the culture of theory, it does not seem to have defined a new subjective cohesion to match the rapidity. Thus the acceleration of time serves to multiply-disintegrate, not to form. The poles of intentionality are lost in this diversity of objects and conditions of production. We are governed by objects that shape our lives according to goals of their own that we cannot make out. What is more, the machine is rapidly accelerating away from us, at the price of our sensibility, our will, our freedom.

Philosophers, those guardians of the universal, must therefore, as far as they are able, reflect upon this destruction of the sensible world that threatens us with individual and collective death, physical and spiritual annihilation. In fact, it is not enough to organize a few more exhibitions, send out a few more messages over the media, produce a few new films, with substantial subsidies, if these cultural manifestations fail to change the status of the universal as a mediation that protects and defends the rights of men and women citizens. Obviously, it is more valuable to invest in culture than in war pure and simple. But war can be waged through art too. An art that does nothing to help life but rather wounds the sensibilities, that exploits them in order to destroy, mobilizes and sollicits them in order to make sterile and perverse, is an immoral art. We can note the negative effects of industry and commerce in the pollution of our senses and the destruction of our environment, in the distractions that constantly assail us in the course of our everyday lives, in the increasing compartmentalization of the workplace as well as in the type of art being produced and exhibited. So many works are designed not to revive us or to bring us together as individuals or groups, but rather to redouble the ill effects we are already suffering at work and in the city. We might expect art to reconfirm the integrity of our body space, but instead this space is invaded and our fields of perception are destroyed. Atomic warfare is played out surreptitiously in our exhibition halls, our museums, in the media, in the artistic environment. Any work that does not seek to bring us together, to afford our perceptions a potential for living unity, is destructive of the *aisthesis*. Such an art blows us apart instead of uniting us as the place where nature and spirit come together.

Art should offer us catharsis and new life, not merely copy a cultural universe that has lost all vitality, all memory that its goal is the universal The task of philosophy is bound up with a concern for art and religion. Philosophy is not useless, as I have heard some philosophers declare. Philosophy is work for the universal that has an individual and a collective utility. A philosophy that is useless has lost its own sense of ethical necessity vis à vis the universal. It is not even folk wisdom. It serves only to irresponsibly abet and even mimic the effects careless technology is having on our lives. When philosophers claim to be useless, perhaps it is because they are afraid. This would be their only excuse, assuming any excuse is possible. But what fear is involved here? And why does the work of thinking induce fear? In today's world we are supposed, even morally obligated, to be frivolous, neurotic, laughable. This is apparently the acceptable tone to be taken by philosophers, a tone that is strangely reminiscent of that kind of entertainment that precedes or accompanies times of great crisis.

Philosophy's job is to work on the universal. But what is there to be done with the universal? Now and always it needs to be thought about. It changes from century to century and the status of the universal is to be a mediation. Now, quite apart from the fact that the universal changes according to the economy of an era, this mediation has never in fact occurred since there has been no thinking about those two halves of the world, men and women. The fear provoked by thinking is probably the fear of a power that is exerted by one part of the world over another. But there would be no place for such disquiet if mediation is thought through and legalized between men and women. The modulatory effects, both on the individual and the collective levels, will be such as to make a unique imperialism impossible.

This universal as a real, not merely a formal, mediation necessarily has some bearing upon the division of social functions: between gathering, farming, and industry, for example. Every tradition tells us that the cultures in which women have a greater share in social life show more respect for the fruits of the earth as sources of food, housing, and clothing. When artificial products replace natural ones this signals the change to a male-oriented society. The process begins when the property of women's genealogies is taken over and capitalized, when food becomes scarce, when new products have to be manufactured for periods of famine. In other words: this begins with the consumption of the other in the place of the consumption of the fruits of the earth. The consumption of the other will take various forms. But the problems of conflict between peoples, between social classes, for example, would not exist if social structures had not been set up that are entirely governed by men, established on the basis of the sacrifice of the other gender, and on a mode of production that goes beyond the potential of the couple, of the family, and of the individual.

Whereas some economists are asking questions along these lines, as do some mythologists and ethnologists, philosophers show no interest and are even hostile to a project they seem to view as a terrible danger, bound up with past history. The reluctance of contemporary philosophers to consider ethical problems, their alacrity in confusing *Moralität* with *Sittlichkeit* seem to correlate with a failure to elaborate any kind of gender ethics or rights. These two do, of course, happen within and between the couple, but we have no cultural, legal, and social representations that mark and maintain this link between *Moralität* and *Sittlichkeit*. I think this is an important task for philosophers. Some technicians, such as Freud, have pointed out some directions to follow, some elements to use as we work on this *Sittlichkeit* on an individual level. More precisely, Freud has told us that the social and the cultural are inseparable from the sexual and that therefore we need to establish ways to sublimate the sexual. This has never been properly thought through or implemented for adult sexuality.

It is fashionable in philosophical circles today to have nothing to do with morality. Such naiveté would be touching if it were not expressed in such a moralizing, repressive, unconstructive tone. We are far from having done with morality, and more particularly with the confusion of the moral with the ethical in sexual difference. For Hegel the individual remains within morality because he is incapable of joining nature and spirit. Hegel reads the nature of right as residing in the people, and he forces each citizen to understand it in this way. I believe that the place and time for the meeting of nature and spirit, of infinite, absolute, and finitude, are located first of all in the sex one belongs to. A balance must be set up within each individual, among all individuals, at each moment and in each place, as we are always faced with the issue of our relationship to a sex that is like or other, that is like and other, that is both.

The leap into the abstract and the undecided, the undecidable, the conditional, the unreal, the necessary imposition of supposedly universal forms are all the result of this lack of the ethical—not the moral, the ethical—between the sexes, always, everywhere, in the intimacy of every relationship, in the theory and practice of public law. For centuries, the scales of justice have tipped heavily one way. The race of men invents all sorts of divisions in the universal that have to be overcome: nature/spirit, State/church, right/left, elected members and candidates, etc., all to avoid addressing the imbalance in rights and duties between men and women. This respect for an elementary justice demands, it is true, that the history of nations be retraced right back to its female legal origins.

Christian painting, art, and religion suggest that we shall have done with morality only after the Last Judgment. In this context I am reminded of certain paintings representing the coronation of the Virgin by Christ the King. Such reciprocity in royal and divine authority seems to have a chance only after the passage beyond all judgment. Does this not mean passing beyond a radical investigation and change in the order of the discourse that authoritatively but arbitrarily and partially lays down the law for us?

FLESH COLORS

Ancona, April 5, 1986
Paper delivered at a seminar on psychoanalysis
organized by the L.A.R.P.

What I am going to try and talk about today, often in the form of questions, stands at the meeting point of the properties of *physical matter* and an elaboration of *sexualized subjective identity* that has still to be thought through and put into practice.

I shall be asking questions with the help of the structure of psychoanalysis. It is definitely in the psychoanalytic context that such issues can best be understood today, given that they do not quite find a home in loving relationships. Often these issues are repressed by problems of social identity, which ignore the fact that the *couple* is the basic social unit. A social thinking that gives no thought to the couple is abstract, cut off from the matter that nourishes it, and perverted by its *abstractness* from addressing the passage from the individual to the race. This passage is eliminated by and within the undifferentiated familial unit that reduces sexual difference to individual and collective reproduction.

So how is a sexualized subjective identity to be constituted, particularly within psychoanalysis?

1. The speed of sound and of light are not at all the same. It appears that psychoanalysis is challenging itself to subordinate the faster of the two to the slower. Light is made to serve sound: everything has to be said, everything has to be passed by sound articulation. Yet Freud insisted that the royal road to the unconscious is the dream, the building of image in which word and text are exceptions.

Since everything has to pass through sound, psychoanalytic practice becomes an exercise in *patience*. If accepted by the patient, the practice is calming, sedative, even soporific, because it is based on the sense of *hearing*. The fantasies, the dreams that are produced in analysis can be partially interpreted as effects of the differences between the speed of light and that of sounds.

These fantasies or dreams are therefore undergone passively, suffered or at least half-suffered. I offer you the hypothesis that they are produced by the energy of a subject who is trying to regain his balance, at least as far as he can. Then the subject risks sinking down and seeing everything go *gray*. Finally he loses all the detail of his perceptions and the sensory contrasts blur. In place of a vivid sensual universe, where the subject can possibly come into existence in his present and his history, there is a demented language without an I (since the I comes out of the perceptions), a system of arbitrary forms whose content is highly problematic. This state of virtual dementia can be induced by depriving the subject of objective sensation or it may occur when the psychoanalytic code and the analyst substitute for sensation a set of pseudoperceptions that have no objective or subjective boundaries.

This implies not an entry into meaning but an entry into *noise*. Seen this way, analysis is threatened by the subject's loss of sense perceptions, and therefore by delirium, paranoia, weakness. . . . In my view, if the patient runs the risk of turning into an idiot through psychoanalysis, it is as a result of sense deprivation and the spiritual dearth that results from the word's inadequacy vis-à-vis sensation and perception.

There is another point to consider: *hearing is also necessary for balance.* When patients are lying down, they feel no occasion to worry about this: hence they are in some danger of losing the bearings they need for balance. This can lead a patient to take off from reality, to construct an artificial reality, to relapse into theoretical delusions, etc. Such delusion is often—or necessarily?—a persecution mania caused by *sense* deprivation. The patient is induced to lose his roots, his balance, and something of his hearing. Such a loss is reminiscent of the most primeval form of regression and persecution. (In this context, it is quite remarkable the way that Schreber confuses the meaning of certain noises and the sound of certain voices with the moment when he separates from his wife and is fascinated by the discourse of medical specialists.)

Thus, psychoanalysis presents a problem of perceptual modification of a very special kind. In my opinion we also need to see that transference is also the result of temporary perceptual disequilibrium given: 1) that the word, the voice, the sense of hearing, are the vehicles chosen for the analyst-analysand relationship; 2) that the patient is lying down.

If we disregard this perceptual imbalance we risk uprooting the patient from his or her body and history. This is equivalent to placing the patient in some abstract, mechanical, neutral energy, turning him or her into a robot with a fabricated history. This energy is created in the way psychoanalysis is set up. If the energy is sustained in the transference as (an artificial) relationship between analyst and analysand, then transference can never be resolved. The only economic outcome is either the destruction of one or both of the robots—with one living off the other, perhaps?—or the quest by certain patients for limits: in illness, death, the passage to action, lateral transferences, etc.

2. What positive action can be taken in analysis to cope with the difference in speed of transmission and perception between sounds and light? The answer I offer you today is: *to paint.* In fact we do this unconsciously and preconsciously *as well,* despite Freud, or the analyst.

The point about painting is to *spatialize perception* and *make time simultaneous,* to quote Klee. This is also the point about dreaming. The analyst should direct his or her attention not only to the repetition of former images and their possible interpretation, but also to the subject's ability to paint, to make time simultaneous, to build bridges, establish perspectives between present-past-future. In psychanalytic therapy it is in my opinion necessarily a question of painting, in this sense. Dreams hint at this and hide it. Which is why dreams are interesting. But the painting must also occur during the session, in the course of every session. In this case, *interpretation* can be defined as the ability to compose along with the patient and to help the patient to paint: to represent his or her perceptions and form them into a perspective in space-time.

If psychoanalytic work and the screening of the unconscious are seen in this way, the analyst must have no abstract and predetermined interpretative paradigm as this may *cut* into the patient's subjectivity. The analyst must help the patient to set up a plan, a framework of simultaneity, a perspective, a depth of field, etc. This also means that the analyst must not *focus* on something too much, unless he or she is sure of doing so in order to create some temporal space. This paradoxical expression highlights a major problem in psychoanalysis. And perhaps in painting too?

Currently, there is considerable emphasis, both in theory and in practice, on the importance of *rhythm,* especially in psychoanalytic interpretation.[1] Rhythm is important. The rhythm of nature that is often referred to is silent or melodic. Other rhythms are often *noisy*. Consequently they risk destroying or effacing the color properties of matter, of perception, of the dream, of the painting. They also threaten to make light and looking submit to sound and listening, both inside and outside. Perhaps this solution expresses a secret nostalgia for the sounds in the womb. Before our birth, we hear many things, particularly our mother's heartbeat. But when we are born we are born to light and to . . . silence.

If a rhythm is imposed from the outside, if we are forced to attend to sounds from the outside, the colors of matter can be erased. So we need to find a balance between hearing, sight, and touch, between sound and light. This can be done with colors. These are also linked to our genetic heritage, and especially our sexual heritage (chromosoma, color-body).

The fact that color is always fading seems to me one of the sources of repression. Repression comes into effect as a result of breaks in rhythm, distinguishing marks, letters, abstract forms, order and laws that are alien to natural growth.

Obviously, it is not possible to suppress rhythm. The important thing is still the harmony and the melody that rhythm allows us to create. Rhythm must facilitate harmony not destroy it.

So the analyst should help the patient to make time simultaneous and then to come to terms with that projection of tenses into the present. Having advocated projection, the analyst must help to get things into perspective and thereby address the patient's symptoms, including those produced by the therapy. A successful analysis would be the one that successfully restores the balance and the harmony of the perceptional economy. Pathology can often be explained by the fact that certain past events and affects are crystallized in the present of the subject, and their energy is no longer available. These residues must be brought to the patient's perception, they must be made fluid again, put in perspective so that creativity can again work freely. This means, for example, that we need to give back to each sense the objective and subjective speeds of its current perceptions and facilitate harmony between these and the past, present, and future history of the subject.

---

1. See, for example, Nicolas Abraham's book *Rythmes: de l'oeuvre, de la traduction, et de la psychanalyse*, Paris: Flammarion, 1985.

Analysis can work to free the patient's energy through the creation of language, not only by playing on words or meanings but also building new linguistic structures—by poetry in the etymological sense of that word. The pun is often an expenditure; it is rarely a structure built to stay. The pun can achieve some permanence when it gives form to culturally free energy, when it seeks an etymology that keeps hold of some unrealized potential, when it discovers a new rhythm.

Building, *poiesis*, is a way of changing forms and rhythm and also, more or less explicitly, colors. An important problem in life is when colors are lost in formal abstractness.

3. Now two things are often forgotten in psychoanalytic theory: the voice, with its different qualities (timbre, intensity, pitch) and colors. These two components of human identity differ according to sex. Certain ideologies say this explicitly and relate these criteria of sexual membership to the properties of the universe. In our patriarchal traditions that favor nonfigurative writing these dimensions are often neglected, and theoreticians have virtually forgotten about them although they remain present in art, at least in certain periods. Thus men and women are not dressed in the same colors. The designation of sex by color is always used to identify divine persons, and this surely tells us that gender or sex is an essential element in the definition of the divine. Colors are also used to separate boy babies and girl babies, though the color code changes oddly from culture to culture. While keeping faith with their color and sound properties the sexes nonetheless escape dichotomic oppositions. Voices and colors cannot be reduced to bipolar couples. Obviously there is a potential bipolarity: blue/red, high/deep. . . . But there are many nuances, variants, and scales of values that move uninterruptedly from one extreme to the other. There are even three or four, not two, so-called primary colors: blue, red, yellow, and green. Thus, these colors do not simply obey binary opposition or one of the principles of noncontradiction that control every truth according to our logical systems. Colors do not obey these rules in their expression of the sexual. They explore all the possible passages and returns from one sex to another, and all the mediations between them. This question of the relation to color is made even more subtle by the fact that we inherit the chromosomes of both sexes and that there is a possible conflict between one's sexualized morphology and one's hormones. This is not to be interpreted as any old bisexuality: each sex inherits

an identity exclusive to itself resulting from its genes, chromosomes, and hormones.

As for sounds, the transitions between high and low are even more obvious. These transitions occur almost imperceptibly. At times there is a switch in the vocal traits associated with each of the sexes. The example of teenage boys comes readily to mind. The switch from high to low is quite sudden and indicates an alternation rather than a simultaneity of possible voice pitches. This is far from a unique case. Each sex retains a whole range of sounds whose chords, mediants, and harmonics must constantly be discovered or recovered as a personal balance or as a relation to the other.

4. In analysis as in other fields it is important to find the economy of the correspondances between sounds and colors, colors and light. In this regard, we need to keep in mind the relation of phonemes to color. The articulations of the letters, as they are pronounced and received, do not correspond to the same colors. There is the pitch of the sounds, their volume, but there is also the shape of the letters. Thus, the labials are dark; the darkest of all is the *m*. The dentals are light. Of the vowels, *a* is chromatically the richest and is called the origin of all colors.[2]

This question of the color of phonemes has been raised by certain poets in regard to vowels. As far as consonants are concerned, I know of no poets who have established letter-color correspondences, but some phoneticians and phonologists have done this for all letters, and there are also philosophers who have taken an interest in the question. It seems that this is a matter of cultural and religious choice.

In any case, the vowels are related to the voice, to sound as song, to color, whereas the consonants are related to articulation and writing. Is color then pronounced but not written? On the other hand, color is painted, it can be seen and contemplated. Color is linked to the voice and to the eye, not to writing as code. Cultures that have nonfigurative writing become cultures without painting in the sense of the artistic expression of sense immediacy. These writing cultures are cultures that lack color as fleshly matter.

How does this happen? Because the body is repressed? Because there is no fleshly spirituality? Because forms—including forms of

2. See, in this context, Roman Jakobson's book *Child Language, Aphasia and Phonological Universals* (The Hague: Mouton, 1968), which includes a very rich bibliography.

law—have been imposed upon sense phenomena? The question of flesh seems to be connected to the question of color. Ultimately, perhaps, flesh is diaphanous, as Aristotle tells us, but it is always taking on and giving colors.

Christianity is one of the cultures of painting, especially when it does not deny its common roots with India, Tibet, Persia. All these are cultures where the gods take flesh and where men-gods are mysteriously born of women known as virgins: Christ is one example, Buddha another.

Their art emphasized color, melodious singing, gestures, figurative symbols. Here color is not subordinate to line. In the end, the incarnation of the divine, of man, of woman, *cannot be imaged without color.* Whereas the signs of writing seek to contain and repress blood, painting and colors try to express blood. The shapes taken by meaning have become arbitrary in our cultures. This arbitrariness splits the subject from his or her body. Meaning ought to express the body and the flesh, not cut itself off from them. The *spatial* representation of the body, of desire, of sensibility has a necessary relation to color. How can we set limits and a time frame to flesh? to color? Of course there are contrasts between colors and relationships that constantly move to find a new balance between their qualities by passing from colder to hotter, from higher to lower. These properties are also forever restoring balance and resolving tensions between the male and female genders. Yellow seems to be the point of mediation between colors and the flesh of the sexes: yellow, sometimes changing to gold, and perhaps green, depending on whether the oppositions and complementarities are divided up in triangles or squares.

Time can thus be made simultaneous by couples in tension, colored couples, sound couples, sexualized couples. Space can be framed in the same way.

As far as the sexual economy is concerned, the issues are very complex and interesting, because in the individual there is always the polarity of sex or gender and the polarity of generation. Tension and harmony between the extremes of colors and sounds exist in each sex to the extent that each person belongs to a gender and is engendered as well as an engenderer. These dimensions are not the same for all. The duality of the sexes allows modifications, transmutations, transpositions, so that a relationship can take place.

Thus in every individual there is:

- genealogical sedimentation with his or her past, present, and future;
- gender or sex as generative seed;
- gender or sex as morphology and identity.

Thus two memories are in tension:

- genealogical memory, always bisexual;
- individual unisexual memory.

Gender as sex is always a transgression of genealogy and of its colors. Memory is always a memory of each individual history; it is also a genealogical memory.

Cultures have forced us to repress the female genealogies. This means that we have entered into a kind of historical mania made up of:

• forms that are balanced in an artificial game of contradictions (the two poles are contained within sameness);

• resemblances, abstracted from the body instead of expressive of it, that form a system of mimicries that allow me to say that I am like the other sex without in fact there being any correspondence with the same living forms, the same relations to sounds, to colors;

• relations that bear no relation to blood, which is loved-hated because it is not rated by its value: blood is repressed because it is associated with female-maternal genealogies. Blood gives rise to fantasies, to a ceaseless cry for wounds that open up the question of life and identity. In turn this leads to racist extravaganzas between peoples, rivalries between individuals, and of course, conflict between the sexes.

The repression that female genealogies have submitted to also seems to have favored codes, privileged writing and all arbitrary forms that seem capable of conveying meaning, doubling the voice, and exacting its submission. Clearly, in the question of writing as art, we are faced with something more than the arbitrariness of the signs. But this other thing is nonetheless linked to a system that reduces the possibility of expression. Writing has difficulty translating colors, sounds, bodily identity, the chromo-soma. . . . All the civilizations that give priority to nonfigurative writing, arbitrary forms, and formal codes, move away from color and from tonality as qualities of flesh, gender, genealogy. They express these as numbers. Mastery and abstraction of the living being?

5. In this context, we need to investigate psychoanalytic theory and practice as methods that assume that sensoriness, affectivity, sexuality, parental relations, individual and collective history can be translated into words. Psychoanalysis submits the flesh to forms alien to those of the body, to its colors, its sounds, its sense dimensions, and it claims in this way to cure the body. It assumes (or deems) it is possible to produce or reproduce everything in words, at best in the form of a narrative, of stories, histories, novels. Clearly, there are dreams and certain fantasies that are like narrative. But how do we dream together? And does dreaming facilitate sexual practice or evade it? Is dreaming a preparation or a substitution for relations between the sexes?

I believe that the style of expression of sex that is permitted by traditional analysis defers or unhinges sexual relations, particularly in their dimension as sexualized gender.

As a result, the sexual act comes to seem impossible and to conform necessarily with certain imperatives: "Have an orgasm," for example.

If color and sounds were manifest, it seems to me that the sexualized dimension of life would be organized in terms of progressively developing rhythms, open stages of space-time, and thus the command "Thou shalt have an orgasm" would not be needed. Such a command operates because of an absence, a repression, or a censorship in the mode of expression.

Psychoanalysts tend to think of memory as layer upon layer of catastrophes: images, words, movements. They rarely define memory as the place where identity is formed, where each person builds his or her own ground or territory. Their idea of memory is negative, in a way. But, as they proceed to intervene in events they class as pathogenic and secondary, psychoanalysts run the risk of undoing the whole fabric of identity. This danger is all the more real because the analytic method of interpretation uses arbitrary, colorless forms and thus catastrophically interrupts the flow of psychic energy.

6. To end or complete an analysis means, in my opinion, to give the other person back his or her power of imagination, that is to say the possibility of receiving—and giving you—the gift of time and space-time.

This cannot be done without imagination. To remain within the limits of the senses in one's suffering or one's jouissance—both of them imaginary—is not the same as acceding to the creation of the imagination. The procedures are different. In the first instance, the senses and the imagination risk destroying one another. In the second, access to the imagination preserves sensitivity: the affect finds a haven within and by means of the imagination. To complete an analysis successfully, as in any other affective relationship, requires access to the art of both sides, access to something fully worked out in the imaginary as well as to something specific to the senses. This entails a specific spatio-temporality that creation alone can keep and develop. The imagination produces symptoms, it is one of the causes of the unconscious, or else it creates a body of work and an identity: either one or the other. The imagination forms a seed around which the past—or its past—crystallizes, or else it opens up a future. All this requires there be a present. This present, in my view, is bound up with perception, or perhaps perceptions, and with the act of creating.

Perception is attention to the present as well as the potential for a future. If I can no longer perceive, I am hallucinating or dead. Sometimes I can survive thanks to the economy of the symbol, particularly the monetary symbol, but I am without the matter and the energy of my body, my senses, my sex. This state of deprivation is what we risk in contemporary society, and in psychoanalysis as part of that society.

7. If Freud considered the psychoanalytic cure to be interminable, it is because he thinks and interprets in terms of *analysis*, not discovery or creation. Defined in this way, analytic work, as I see it, seems to occur *outside of time* and to expose the subject to destruction by producing an artificial time frame subordinate to the spoken word and to transference. An exclusively analytic frame of reference stands in the way of psychic discovery, synthesis, and integration. The work of analysis destroys, deconstructs, and allows no room for resynthesis. Synthesis can come only out of the *imagination*, not the faculty of analysing. If the imagination is cathected solely in an effort of analysis, the subject's space-time is destroyed, annihilated, or perverted. It is forced to undergo infinite sections and divisions, sometimes it is sidetracked, but it can no longer live in itself because it lacks a subjective synthetic function. When, with the help of various appropriate techniques, the subject is reduced (pricked, punched, perforated) to an infinite heap of fragments, a supposedly unlimited collection of dots, subjectivity is destroyed, sensitivity and affect

yield before the simple *urge* to know *more*, before a *belief* in knowing more, which is shared by the analyst.

But why is there such a desire to know? Knowledge alone cannot constitute the unity of the subject; in fact it tends rather to splinter the subject, or even force its obedience to some absolute cause. Furthermore, the knowledge we gain from analysis is probably man's weakest resource if it is cut off, on the one hand, from a receptive affect or sensoriness, and, on the other, from the imagination as synthetic faculty. This faculty is disintegrated and threatened with internal and external gregariousness: one + one + one . . . resulting from a limitless scission or dispersion, multiples that have no horizon or point of assembly in the flesh.

8. In this abstractness, if we can actually call it such, analysis loses sight of the sexual dimension, which cannot be equated to an infinitely divisible materiality. That which is sexed is linked to perception, to its specific imaginary creation as well to regeneration, procreation, and more generally, life.

In analysis the subject is often reduced to the passive object of a hypothetical Other. In this way the subject can be cut up into infinite bits with no remainder. Why with no remainder? Because it has isolated itself within the faculty of analysis and abandoned the other faculties: perceiving, imagining, dreaming. If I devote all my energies to a faculty that has no resources behind it—as is the case with the faculty of analysis—I can never find myself in front of anything. I have even destroyed the object that I was.

I feel that subjective liberation and development mandate a method that is still ill defined because we lack an imagination capable of creating the sex, the flesh. To fill that lack, we need to put perception and creation into relation with art, with aesthetic perspectives, forms, colors, and especially with the play of contrasts.

We need to have two in each sex, not one sex divided between two. Perception and creation differ from one gender to the other. When we divide perception and creation between the two genders we impoverish both and destroy the identity of each. This false division ends up by changing human faculties: perception becomes sensation and the imagination becomes an imaginary that corresponds to a *pathos* of the senses.

If certain psychoanalysts appear unaware of the difference between the sexes this is because they place themselves, perhaps unconsciously, within a methodology that is far too narrow, which had

potential at a certain point in history and arose out of certain tendencies at that time. That method augurs ill for the future of the
subject in that it has no resources of its own, is not founded within
itself, and makes its appearance at perhaps the most impoverished
time in the development of the spirit. In this context we need to
remember that sexual difference is not to be recognized only from
signs or signifiers that have already been coded, which are, in any
case, far from unchanging. Sexual difference also corresponds to the
possibility of different perceptions and creations.

Strangely enough, one perception that culture has clung to is that
man keeps sight, the gaze, the reflection (Narcissus) for himself and
allows woman to keep hearing and the echo (Echo). In order to
repeat one needs to have first heard. Now, in the East, the ear is
considered to be the most sensitive of all the organs, and it is also
known as the female organ. Furthermore, some theories put forward
the hypothesis that the ear is the place on which is inscribed the
movement whereby the fetus in the final months of pregnancy turns
itself head down. Could it be that woman, as mother, ceaselessly
operates this turnaround?

From the point of view of the relation of colors, I can thus put
forward the hypothesis that woman must convert sounds into colors,
and man colors into sounds, or light into sounds. Between the two of
them the whole range of colors and sounds comes into play. Each of
them stands at one end of the range and has to work together with
the other to realize the whole harmony, but without leaving hold of
this or her genetic identity, which is the condition of life for each as
individual as well as the force that attracts each to the other.

9. Hysteria has been and is still the source of energy that has not
been coded—the flesh, the seed of analysis. Hysteria stands between
woman and mother, women and mothers. It is in tension between
them. Hysteria must not be destroyed but allowed access to the
imagination and to creativeness. For the hysteric access to such an
identity is effected through a sexualized art, a colored and sonorous
art, an art whose libidinal resources blossom in duality and reconciliation, within one woman, between mother and wife, and among
women. Thanks to such an art, the hysteric should be able to regain
her perceptions—her virginity, her gender—and keep hold of them.
Creativity is a goal only for someone who gives priority to *making
an object*, to anality (?). For the sublimation of genitality—a dimension that is still unknown to us, particularly because it has been

buried beneath the idea that reproduction is our duty as women and the sole way we can achieve our sexuality—artistic creation represents a means, not an end. This is the indispensable road to take not only for psychoanalysis but, more generally, in every relationship, if we are to realize an art of the sexual that respects the colors, the sounds, and the forms proper to each sex.

This imperative solves the dilemma of art for art's sake. If art is a necessary condition for the establishment of a culture of affective relationships, and especially sexual relationships, then art is useful as a place where individual, bodily matter can be transmuted and sublimated. Art is not just an aid to a social body that has already been abstracted from the sexual dimension, though these are the traditional terms of the debate.

Without art, sexuality falls into a natural immediacy that is bound up with reproduction and into infinite particles. We women have either forgotten or we never learned the art of genital sublimation, perhaps because of a historic gap between the culture that corresponds to female genealogies and the culture produced by the social foundations of patriarchy. It may be that the female and male genders have never made cultural contact within that tradition. This is the strongest hypothesis I can advance to explain why this issue of vital importance to the individual and to culture is habitually met with a blind eye and a deaf ear.

THE THREE GENDERS

Florence, May 11, 1986
Conference organized by the Centro documentazione
donna and the Libreria delle donne: Il viaggio

A. The notion of gender

The structure of discourse and its impact on meaning, the truth it translates and transmits, is still a subject that is relatively little analyzed and even more rarely identified as an *instrument* used in all of the sciences.

The sciences are forever polishing new instruments, developing new machines (all very expensive, moreover!), but very little thought or research is devoted to the ultimate technique—language—the ultimate tools—words. Except perhaps when it is a question of programming computers?

We have been told that man is the talking animal. Today, man seems ready for machine brainpower to make the decisions about his biological, affective, intellectual, social present, and future. . . .

A strange era where "cold" hypertechnicity is accompanied by a rather worrisome obsession with irrational passions and ancient country magic. Medecine, with all its resources is called upon to treat the problem. As for religion per se, who knows?

In this crisis of irrationality should we not be seeing signs that our culture and our time are changing? Is it feeling the urge to develop a new discourse? particularly in the relations between the microcosm and macrocosm? Between us and the universe, but also within us and among us, we have to think up another world.

Hence my project of working on *gender* in discourse:

—Gender as index and mark of the *subjectivity* and the ethical responsability of the speaker. In fact gender is not just a question of biology and physiology, a matter of private life, of animal habits or

The Women's Documentation Center and the Women's Bookstore, The Journey.—Tr.

vegetal fertility. It constitutes the irreducible differentiation that occurs *on the inside of "the human race."* Gender stands for the unsubstitutable position of the *I* and the *you* (*le tu*) and of their modes of expression. Once the difference between *I* and *you* is gone, then asking, thanking, appealing, questioning . . . also disappear.

It seems that, instead of becoming more of a man by developing the sexualized morphology of his discourse, man today is committed to keeping himself out of language, no longer saying *I* or *you* or *we*. The sciences, technological practices, certain ways of regressing into religiosity all fit into this pattern. By taking over from the *I* (here and now) of the subject and from some potential *you*, these other kinds of truth can make up the rules.

—Hence my second investigation. Not to say *I* means surrendering our words, our voice to some agent that is supposedly more worthy to articulate our truth. What is it about this agent that makes it better able to speak than we? To speak in a *universal* and *neuter* way? Does neutrality exist? Where? How?

If I begin to question discourse—beginning with the language that I speak and that has made me a subject—I shall observe that the neuter is apparently a matter of *nature* in the first instance. Expressions like "it is raining," "it is snowing," "it is windy," "it is thundering" . . . refer to powers (*puissances*) that resist human power (*pouvoir*) and its formalization. This is no inert matter that opposes and imposes upon man, but an *animate* nature that is spoken of rather whimsically and that is today translated by the *neuter:* in its movements, its manifestations, its rhythms as well as when we become aware of it: "that smells good," "that is so beautiful," "there goes the thunder" . . . In the last resort, the sense that could turn things round is *touch*, our body as a *tactile instrument* for apprehending and manipulating the world, ourselves, the other. This instrument is a manual instrument but also a speech instrument: translation, relay, creation. Does this work of man—and I say "man" advisedly since it is men who for centuries have been working actively to manipulate and transform the universe by means of their hands, of tools, and of language—seek to do as nature does? to mimic her? impose itself as a power (*puissance*) without any subjective gender mark? Thus we would move from the "it is sunny" or "it is raining" (two phrases that set up a rhythm rather than establishing a formal dichotomy) to "it is necessary," "it is true," "this is how it is," or not. This order of laws is intended to be neuter but carries the brand of the man who produced it. Between the time of the seasons and weather and historical time, there is the time of the creation of the worlds, of the installation of their economy, and of the gods or of a God speaking in nature.

Three "its," three so-called neuters need investigation: the language of nature, the word of the exclusively male god(s), the cultural order and its discourse through things. Through machines? Things of our era that command a language that sometimes overwhelms us, annihilates us, and whose noise can be heard loud and clear over the sound of the silence of the natural order.

This can be said in another way: most of the time, language serves as a vehicle for meaning, for content. How has discourse authorized this content, this meaning, this culture? How can it set up others? These aspects of the message are rarely questioned.

Hence my decision to investigate the structure of discourse, the language instrument, in order to interpret sexualization and seek to shift its order. This work has to be carried out on two levels of discourse:

—the level at which, consciously or unconsciously, it formalizes its means, its powers;

—the level of style, of the subjective involvement of the speaker, and the speaker's relation to the body, to gender.

In fact, it is necessary to analyze the relation in discourse between:

• that which can be formalized, passively/actively, popularly/scientifically, etc.
• that which as style resists formalization.

This involves developing the problem of ethical responsibility in relation to formalization, but also the problem of the expression or translation of identity into style. Is the one separable from the other? Does the element of sexual difference not act as a *brake upon* and a *store of resistance against* a formalization that threatens life, against an ill-considered development of science and technology that result in bodily paralyses? This project is not only a matter of doing justice to one sex but also of responsibly preserving and establishing the consciousness and the creation of life, of the world. Such a task demands that we take account of the responsibility of the speaker, that we question the discourse that claims to be indifferent to the subject—in its dimensions of perceptions, sensitivity, intelligence,

171

sexuality—that assumes universality and neutrality. What is hidden by the neuter? Where does gender get hidden in the economy of discourse? How can gender be uncovered?

In order to get close to the sex dimension of discourse, it is not enough to shift its rules and change its propositions about content, especially historical content. We need to analyze very rigorously the forms that authorize that content. If the ethical, or even merely cultural, transformation in our attitudes toward sexual difference is never achieved or else is botched, this is because we are failing to effect an *active* shift in the laws and in the order of discourse.

B. THE UNCONSCIOUS TRANSLATION OF GENDER INTO DISCOURSE

I must emphasize that I am not going to define an ideal model of language. This means that I am not claiming to isolate in any *absolute* way the most important elements in the language spoken by men and by women. I can speak only of what I have observed. In any case I have no desire to set up a *fixed* and *immutable* paradigm of the production of discourse; my goal is to show that the generation of utterances is not neuter but sexualized. Sexual difference has always served procreation. For some time now, sexual difference has not played a part in the *creation of culture*, except in a division of roles and functions that does not allow both sexes to be subjects. Thus we are confronted by a certain *subjective pathology* from both sides of sexual difference. This pathology shows more or less clearly in patterns of social behavior. It is covered over by different masks and there is great resistance to analyzing or even acknowledging this pathology, either because the language is considered as an ideal that is alien to the body producing it, or because it is said to be reduced to the superstructure of a restricted economy. There are other possible hypotheses, notably the theory that sexualized language is subject to repression or censorship. Even people who profess to be be sexually liberated (either in the therapeutic mode or else in direct political activities) often refuse to accept that language is sexualized. Such persons look no further than content and certain sexual representations, and they ignore the fact that sexualization corresponds to a general structure of discourse.

The sexualization of discourse is indeed not a matter of a few words here and there, even though the fact that certain words do not exist in the *lexicon* can be structurally significant. Similarly, the *gender markers* of some languages (masculine, feminine, neuter) do not exhaust the way sex generates significance in utterances, although they are revelatory of social and historical phenomena. Gender markers show how one sex, how the world, has been forced to submit to the other. Thus, at least in French, the masculine gender always carries the day syntactically: a crowd of a thousand persons, nine hundred and ninety-nine women and one man will be referred to as a masculine plural; a couple composed of a man and a woman will be referred to in the masculine plural; a woman telling the story of her love affair with a man will have to use the supposedly neutral masculine plural form in her agreement of past participles when she says "we fell in love" (*nous nous sommes aimés*), etc. In other places, the neuter is expressed by the same pronoun as the masculine: *il tonne* ("it is thundering") and *il faut* ("it is necessary") not *elle* tonne or *elle* faut. These laws of syntax in French reveal the power wielded by one sex over another.

This same sex has in fact taken over the most highly valued truths: *God* in most, or even all, languages today is a masculine noun; so is *sun*; in those countries where the moon is important, moon too is a masculine noun. Man gives his own gender to the universe as he intends to give his name to his children and his possessions. Everything man considers of value has to be of his gender. The feminine is a marker of secondariness, of subordination to the principal gender. The *neuter* is reserved for specific and variable areas in different languages. Analysis of the origins of the neuter often indicates that it arises after sexual difference has been eradicated. Thus, cosmic phenomena, once the attribute of gods *and goddesses*, are translated today in the neuter: it is snowing, it is raining, it is sunny, etc. Each of these acts was once associated with a male or female power. Similarly, the *it is necessary, it behooves* constructions we have inherited from the Greeks or from Greek philosophers probably hide a reference to a sexual imperative, a gendered fate that had power over gods and humans. Subsequently, this *it is necessary* was incorporated into Roman law. But laws have been made by men alone. The *it is necessary* refers to a duty or an order that has been laid down by one sex only, one gender only. It has only the appearance of being neuter or neutral, and in French at any rate it has the same form as the masculine.

Our social organizations and the discourse that arises out of them are thus regulated by a neuter that is controlled by the masculine gender. Serving as neutral ground for the wars and quarrels among men, this neuter does not solve the problem of the hierarchy observed by the male and female genders, of the injustices this hierarchy perpetuates or the pathogenic neutralization of languages and values that results.

This centuries-old taboo on a truly sexualized morphology of and in culture leads to repressions, compensations, and pathologies. Hence the invention of various forms of individual and collective therapy. Psychoanalysis is the most obvious example of these, and, given the way it sets up the therapeutic stage and the way it relies on language for its cure, psychoanalysis is also the place where the troubles with language show up most clearly. It is is within the nonsocial context of the analytic session that the difference in the structure of utterance among subjects can be seen most simply. If I take traditional classifications as my starting point, it seems that patients labeled hysteric and those labeled obsessional do not use the same structures of discourse. Hysterics (or at least female hysterics) generate utterances of the type: (I) ← Do you love me? → (you) or (I) ← I like what you like → (you). Obviously, this is not a simple example of what one immediately hears said. This is a model sentence gained by analysing several bodies of recorded utterances and reducing them to kernel phrases, etc.[1] The obsessional patient, on the other hand, produces this type of discourse: (I) ← I tell myself that perhaps I am loved → (you) or (I) ← I wonder if I am loved → (you). For the hysteric, the message, the object exchanged, the vision of the horizon in the world, tend to belong to the *you* whereas for the obsessional they belong to the *I*. The objection that there are female obsessives and male hysterics is not a valid one. The hysteric male model is different from the hysteric female one. The same is true for the female obsessive.[2]

But sexual difference can also be found within certain so-called homogeneous groups. Thus, female *schizophrenics* do not work out their own idiosyncratic codes in the same way as male schizophrenics. Women are concerned with a corporal geography whereas men establish new linguistic territories.

The sexualized structure of discourse can be found in areas that have not been defined as pathological in any way. Thus, students of

1. See the essay "Grammaire de l'énonciation de l'hystérique et du obsessionnel," in my recently published collection, *Parler n'est jamais neutre* (Paris: Editions de Minuit, 1985).
2. See the essay "L'ordre sexuel du discours" in the special issue dedicated to "Le sexe linguistique" in the journal *Langages*, March 1987, published by Larousse.

different sexes, when presented with the same trigger words, do not produce the same phrases. Not only the content but the form of their utterances is different. In the phrases that I have analyzed in my research, the words given the students were: marriage, celibacy, maternity, paternity, femininity, for example. The results of the studies were collected by a team of people working on obstetrical prophylaxis.[3] The authors of these studies gained results significantly different from mine. It is true that their goal was to study the content and not the structure of the discourse. In my opinion, the phrases produced by men and women differ in the choice of subjects, of verbs, of tenses, of moods, of transformations operated upon the predicate, etc. This can be interpreted as showing that the subject who generates the utterance is adopting a different position toward language, the object of discourse, the world, the other. Contrary to what is usually said and understood, women construct more objective phrases, whose meaning or denotation is sustained by largely extralinguistic contexts. The utterances of the men are much more connotative. They affirm their subjective imprint in an often passionate way ("I lay claim to the paternity of these sentences" one of the men answers when faced with the word *paternity*) whereas the women, who have the reputation of being incapable of objectivity, reply in a much more impersonal manner, a much more "scientific" style. Such results may seem surprising. They match those gathered in a psychoanalytic context, however. On the male side, the *I* is affirmed in different ways and is significantly more stressed than the *you* or the *world*. On the female side, the *I* tends to leave some space for the *you* and the *world*, for the objectivity of words and things. From this point of view, women seem to be better listeners, more able to discover and manage the other and the world, more open to *objective* invention and creation, as long as they are also able to say *I*.

I have just given two examples of the role of sex in discourse. In my work, I have approached the issue of the sexual order of culture from various angles: the different utterances of the hysteric and the obsessional, the production of sentences by male and female students, Freud's theory *about* Dora, the text that Schreber addresses *to* his wife, the sexual language of legends and folk tales, the way in which the discourse of science, philosophy, art and religion have been shaped by gender (see the essays in this present collection and

3. See *Bulletin de la Societe nationale de Psychoprophylaxie obstetricale*, 1971, pp. 21–40.

in my other books; my studies on Dora and Schreber have yet to be published).

When we analyze the expressions of the subject in language, visual images, art, legends, myths, we discover that *sex is a primary and elementary dimension of subjective structure.* We are sexed beings and we produce sexed forms. Of this production—not just reproduction—in difference, we know very little, but we have an ever greater need to guard against a technocratic imperialism that cares little about the regeneration of the living world, of freedom, of the future. This also implies that sexual difference is essential if we are to use our technical powers to build human values, rather than to destroy them.

For me, working on language is not simply a matter of preparing statistical studies or establishing what is the state of affairs. I make use of scientific machinery in order to bring to light certain tendencies that are habitually hidden and forgotten. But can we speak and be conscious of the form, or forms, of what we say? This is not certain! Sometimes, in fact, it seems impossible. Whence, the need to pursue the investigation.

The project is to uncover who speaks, to whom, about what, with what means. In technical terms this entails uncovering the dynamics of discourse that underlie individual utterances. Underneath what is said, we can uncover the subject, its economy, its relations with the world and the other, its potential energy. The subject is masked, engulfed, buried, covered over, paralyzed, or else it generates, engenders, becomes, develops, grows, while speaking.

To work on the sexhood of languages thus means revealing who the *I, you, he, she* are in the discourse of men and women. This enables us to interpret why domestic, social, and cultural relations between the sexes so often get bogged down in misunderstandings and so often reach a dead end. This type of work allows us to analyze the symptom, to name and understand the illness, to find the openings that enable us to modify the economy of utterance and of social intercourse in general. A formalism that has been merely suffered and produced unconsciously can in this way become a style.

C. THE EXPRESSION OF GENDER IN A STYLE

Some people will find this work rather dry, even if it has its entertaining and stimulating intellectual moments. Therefore I now want to talk about another thing that motivates me and that I think is very important. No narrative, no commentary on a narrative, are enough to produce a change in discourse. If anything they risk repressing sexual and affective freedom by moralizing—unless, that is, they can manage to create a style, unless they go beyond the utterance into the creation of new forms. In this context I am thinking of all the autobiographical narratives of today that have not been transposed into novels, short stories, legends, theories. This transformation of the autobiographical *I* into a different cultural *I* seems essential if we are to set up a new ethics of sexual difference. If we are not to run the risk of producing a traditional moral code—abstract norms for experience, formal frameworks, or a truth that emerges from the personal experience of someone who happens to shout louder than all the others—then it is equally crucial that we not qualify that ethics with an explanation of what is being invented and discovered therein as acts of creativity, love, freedom. Two procedures are important for setting up different norms for life: the analysis of the formal structures of discourse on the one hand and the creation of a new style on the other. Thus, in my book *Ethics of Sexual Difference*, which relies on a large number of earlier cultural analyses (see *Speculum of the Other Woman*, *This Sex That Is Not One*, *Marine Lover*, *L'oubli de l'air*, the greater part of the essays in *Parler n'est jamais neutre*), there is no basic narrative, no possible commentaries by others, in the sense of an exhaustive decoding of the text. What is said in those books moves through a double style: a style of loving relationships, a style of thought, of exegesis, of writing. The two are consciously or unconsciously linked, with a more immediately corporeal and affective side in one case, a more socially developed side in the other. But the language there is already allied with others. And an alliance is not easily transposed outside of its act. An alliance with language is the same.

The movements that are choreographed according to a certain style do not make up a formal model. Even when it is captured by fashion, imitated, caricatured, robbed of a part of its content, a style remains irreducible. It is not susceptible of reduction to a grill that may be transposed or imposed elsewhere. A style resists coding, summary, counting, cataloguing, programming into different machines. It cannot be brought down to the level of such oppositions as sense/mind, poetry/ideas . . . masculine/feminine, as these dichotomies have been presented to us so far. A style cannot be reduced to bipolar alternatives: positive/negative, better/worse, etc. It may accommodate them, especially in the commentaries (digests?) that in different ways contradict its purpose, but style escapes all of these because it creates without resolving or dissolving into dichotomies, however sophisticated they may be.

Hence the resistance? What is resistance? What does it say exactly? What already existing meaning is involved? Such questions remain unanswered, they lack a context and this can raise the objection that the thinking is esoteric. But every text is esoteric, not because it hides a secret but because it constitutes the secret, that which has yet to be revealed is never exhaustively revealable. The only response one can make to the question of the meaning of the text is: read, perceive, experience. . . . *Who are you?* is probably the most relevant question to ask of a text, as long as one isn't requesting a kind of identity card or an autobiographical anecdote. The answer would be: *how about you?* Can we find common ground? talk? love? create something together? What is there around us and between us that allows this?

We cannot achieve this without the horizon of sexual difference. No world is produced or reproduced without sexed difference. Plants, animals, gods, the elements of the universe, all are sexed.

The theory that the mere force of matter (what force? and what are we calling matter?) engenders organized beings remains a pressing issue, especially when we consider the origins of human life. The research being done to prove this hypothesis is deep and extensive and often neglects our most elemental realities and needs. But so far no one can claim to belong to a universe that has one sex or no sex. Except in fiction, perhaps? and in certain formal truths of science that have been abstracted from life and are called neutral?

Man seems to have forgotten this, the most universal as well as the most creative part of his destiny. In the beginning "God" (or some animal or vegetable couple) created us naked, man and woman, in a garden that gave us all the food and shelter we needed. Laboring to earn a living, laboring to give birth, marks an *exile* from this garden. The toil that has become our lot, *our only horizon*, is, then only an exile, a waiting to return. The ban on the flesh, the obligation to work and to suffer, are the reverse image, the failure of our first birth. Today man is combing through his archeology of myths, when he is not going out to search for himself in the most distant planets. But all the while he is bound here and now by a *fault* he can never be free of, and for which he can never substitute a third party, such as love, grace, the jubilation of the flesh and the share these have in language too.

One apochryphal gospel records Christ telling a certain Salome that happiness will return to earth only when women cease to bear children! This could be understood to mean that when love has been discovered the child is no longer *necessary*. But the text, or texts, add that then sexual difference will be effaced. This is as much as to say that sexual difference existed only for and by the child, and within the hierarchy: there will be no more man or woman, nor master or slave.

If sexual difference is to be overcome is it not imperative first of all to find a sexual ethics? If one day we are to be one must we not now be *two*? Otherwise we fall back into some formal and empty (*male) one*, back into the hierarchies we are familiar with, or into a nostalgia for returning back into the womb where the other is nothing but an encompassing source of food and shelter. In his travels has man not mixed the most ancient of the earth with the most heavenly of the skies?

How has sexual ethics come to be so neglected? Why is it approached in such a roundabout fashion, through animal ecology, the sexhood of plants, the more or less pathological language of our cells, the sex of our chromosomes, of our brain, etc? Sexuality seems to have become a stake in some power play, or else a source of suffering, nothing much more. . . . Man no longer even takes time out to make a sexual display. He has to work faster, ever faster. As for woman, her moves as a lover have still to be invented. She has got lost in her role as mother, or else in a sexual display that does not really match her space of meeting and embracing. She may possibly manage to express her need-desire to be loved, but not her love. Why? Woman's value has been equated solely with her capacity to bear and to nurture a son, and to the language that corresponds to that function. Man, who, through his work, has a monopoly on the symbolic, has given no thought to his body or his flesh. And, apart from the fact that man needs to give his thoughts to himself, he might have had some trouble in saying what constitutes the particularity of the female sexual world: a different energy, a different morphology, a special relation to mucus and to the threshold that goes from inside to outside the body, from the inside to the outside of the skin (and the universe?) without leaving a wound.

Thus, for women, the issue is to learn to discover and inhabit a different kind of magnetism and the morphology of a sexualized body, particularly of the mucus particularities and qualities of that body. But women's flesh (and is not mucus in great measure the matter of which flesh is made?) is still ignored, often imagined as chaos, abyss, or rebus. Whether as prime matter or as creation's reject, woman has yet to find her forms, yet to spread roots and bloom. She has yet to be born to her own growth, her own subjectivity. The female has yet to develop its own *morphology*. Forced into the maternal role, reduced to being a womb or a seductive mask, the female has served only as the means of conception, growth, birth, and rebirth of *forms* for the other.

But how can one marry that which has no *forms?* no edges? no limits? no style of marriage and alliance to propose? As long as woman fails to affirm herself, man drowns, consumes, or undertakes some nostalgic odyssey. Woman, for her part, mothers her little son, her little outside self: she makes him grow and flourish in her place. As wife, she masks and clothes herself. But this display, even if unintentional, is nothing but a web of deception. The garment that is assumed only *for the other*, that is not an expression of my flesh, unveils a kind of nothingness once it is removed: woman's inability to love herself, to care for herself, to become a partner *other*, someone who is not simply what man expects her to be, and therefore always desirable and attractive. She can be beautiful, with a beauty that is not just a surface creation, but an emanation of her inner being, her intimate self. Such words may make people laugh today, but they carry weight in many other traditions where they designate an energy that can be maintained.

In our tradition we women perhaps miss the experience of discovering and living our initiation into sexuality *together*. In certain cultures men in groups ritually celebrate the experience of passing into manhood. In one way or another such rites continue in our own cultures. For women this initiation into sexuality is a solitary event, even when it is observed. The little girl becomes a wife or a mother alone, or at best with her mother or some substitute. Even when women are together, they rarely know how to live and speak of that passage from one state to another. They compain about what's been happening lately, they compete, they bitch, they worry out loud.

They rarely initiate one another into their developing roles as women. Possibly they talk of their experiences in childbirth or about their mothers. Of their sexual needs and desires they speak almost not at all. If they do so it is usually in terms of the wrongs done them, the hurts suffered. Women exchange bits and pieces of games that have already been played. They rarely invent new games, games *of their own*.

Language seems to have paralyzed us, frozen even our words. Though adults, we have no mobility. Once chidlhood is over, we can move only along the paths of poetry, art, prayer. The fact that female intelligence is still *silent* surely means that there are *movements* that must still be set free. The issue for women is not to go one better than technology, even if this were in their power, but to discover gestures that have been forgotten, misunderstood, gestures that are also words, that are different from the gestures of maternity and shed a different light upon generation in the body, in the strict sense of the term.

The least remembered symbol in the universe and in our cultures is the sexual symbol, *living symbol*. Failing to understand this living symbol, men—only men—exchange women, children, manufactured goods, passwords, coins (many of which bear female images?). Men exchange some *thing* instead of exchanging love, god(s), art, thought, language. Any statement claiming that God is the most noble human exchange possible, constitutes the celestial keystone to man's edifice, is the foundation of language, has no strength if God is not really exchanged. Now, for many centuries, God has been given a monopoly of truth(s) and ritual. But God has always one negative predicate: invisibility. As invisible as the relationship between the sexes, in large part, as the act of intercourse, particularly through the mediation of woman. What birth is taking place, is as yet to come, between these two poles of invisibility? How are we to uncover and interpret the traces they leave in discourse? How are existing languages to be remodeled so as to give place to a sexed culture? These are the issues targeted by my research.

A CHANCE FOR LIFE

Limits to the concept of the neuter
and the universal in science
and other disciplines

Tirrenia, July 22, 1986
Festival of women of the Italian Communist Party,
organized around the theme:
"Life after Chernobyl"

The accident that occurred at Chernobyl has created a general furor. Whether consciously or not, most men and women have viewed this accident as the most extreme example of world disorder. Once it had in fact been possible to hope that the confusion and entropy characteristic of our era might, at least in the last resort, be controlled by nature. This is a serious scientific hypothesis, it is something that shows the reign or the sociopolitical influence of women, it is the most generous solution for the whole world, and the goal that millions of people strive for, more or less blindly, as they cling to some little patch of ground as to their last hope of salvation.

But, at Chernobyl, nature turned into a vehicle of destruction that went beyond any weapon of war. This means that both of the solutions designed to reduce disorder have now been put into question: both *nature* and *war*. We can no longer assume that nature will fulfill its role as regulator of our energies and our lives, as individuals and as collectives, now that the risk of pollution has become mortal and worldwide. And war can no longer be waged as a specific policy tool since it cannot be contained within the limits of a declared conflict.

Some women panicked when they were faced with the twofold pollution of manmade things and natural phenomena: hail, storm, even sun. Others felt that we must guard against a fear of nature despite all the warnings given in the media. Many became convinced that the cultural disorder we have embarked upon willy-nilly has become intolerable.

Since May I have met many women and men who are physically or mentally sick. We don't exactly know, I think, what is wrong with us, with our bodies, with nature as a whole. All the same, it is possible to say that disorder has been increased by the pollutions, the illnesses, the acts of desperation and panic. So we need to take some fairly simple but rapid cultural measures to try and get our culture back into balance. In fact it's not just a question of Chernobyl. This accident, which could have been predicted either in one place or another, is just one symptom of a series of facts about our culture: practical facts and theoretical facts. I shall only cite a few as I do not wish to sadden you during this holiday period. But ignorance, when mixed with fear, also casts a shadow. It is better to be a little forewarned and able to make some objective decisions, however small.

What does it mean that our culture is threatened with destruction? Of course, there are the obvious threats posed by war, since warfare is the only way of assuring international equilibrium—or so we are informed by the media, whose economy might bear investigation.

I shall return to this point. So the death machines are traded around with vast capital expenditures, and all to keep the peace, or so they tell us. This warrior way of organizing society is of patriarchal origin. Things don't have to work this way. This all comes down to sex. But the era of high technology has given weapons of war a power (*puissance*) that goes beyond the conflicts and risks that patriarchs have liked to indulge in. Women, children, every living thing, even elementary matter, now have a stake in the war machine. And death and destruction are not merely the outcome of war. They are found in the physical and mental assaults we have to cope with permanently every day. What we need is a general cultural change and not just a decision concerning war as such. Patriarchal culture is a culture founded upon sacrifice, crime, and war. It lays upon every man the duty and the right to fight for food and shelter, to defend his possessions, and his family and country as possessions. A decision about war from the patriarchy is necessary at this point but it will fall far short of providing a cultural mutation. The race of men make war everywhere all the time with a perfectly good conscience. Man is traditionally carnivorous, even cannibalistic. Therefore he has to kill to eat, enslave nature more and more in order to live and survive, journey to the farthest stars to find something that no longer exists here on earth, defend by any means available his own little satrapy. Men are always plunging deeper and deeper into exploitation and plunder—without understanding very well why. Men go out in search of something they imagine they need without questioning who they are and the relationship between what they do and their identity.

To address such failures of understanding, I believe that the race of men needs the help of persons whose function would be to promote self-understanding among men and to set limits. Only women could fill this function. Women do not belong to the patriarchal culture as fully responsible subjects. Hence they have the potential to interpret this culture in which they have fewer vested interests and involvement than men and in which they themselves are not so much products of the system as to be blinded by it. Operating on the outside, women can offer a more objective view of society since they have been relatively excluded from it. Furthermore, women are not, in principle, supposed to be in a hierarchical relation with men. All other minority groups are caught up in such hierarchies. And it is with a completely patriarchal, unconscious or cynical condescension that politicians and theoreticians interest themselves in such minorities and exploit them, with all the risks of the possible reversals of the master-slave relations. This dialectic—or absence of dialectic— has been inscribed, since the very beginning of the patriarchy, in father-son relations. As a path to freedom and peace it is doomed to failure because it is based: (1) upon *genealogy*, with no balancing influence coming from a horizontal relation between the genders; (2) on *male genealogy alone*, which rules out any possibility of forming a dialectic between the genealogies and the male and female genders.

Our only chance today lies in a cultural and political ethics based upon sexual difference. In economics and religion, the world is barely keeping its balance. Furthermore, the developments in technology subject us to such harsh ordeals that we are threatened with physical and mental annihilation. We have neither the time nor the leisure to think, however much spare time we are given, and we are endlessly negligent, forgetful, distracted. But the science of men cares less about prevention or the present than about healing. With the objective purpose of accumulating material possessions and with the subjective goal of bolstering the male subjective economy, science allows disorder and pollution to increase and funds various kinds of curative medicine. Science contributes to destruction, then repairs things as best it may. But a body that has suffered is never the same. It retains the traces of physical and moral trauma, it remembers despair, thirsts for revenge, falls into apathy. This whole economy is testimony to the way men have forgotten life, denied the debt they owe to their mothers and their maternal genealogy, to the women who carry out the work of producing and sustaining life. Vast resources are squandered for money. But what is money if it does not serve life? Despite the various probirth policies that nations adopt for economic or sometimes religious reasons, it is clear that destroying life is as much an imperative as giving birth.

187

How are we to minimize this contradiction, which lies at the heart of most of our societies? It cannot be solved unless we trace it back to its patriarchal roots. We live in a society of intermale bondings, which respects only the genealogy of the sons and the fathers and the competition among brothers. This means that our societies have subordinated women's genealogy to men's. The daughters are separated physically and culturally from their mothers when they have to move into their husbands' families and male institutions. The family, strictly defined, the schools, the workplace, commerce, the States, the information systems, even most of of our leisure activities are organized according to a male economy and male rights. Division by sex, which represents one of the essential characteristics of living matter, has not been fostered in our society for centuries, and the technological era we are living through now aims to eliminate it. I am not simply referring to methods of artificial reproduction but to the whole mass of mechanical conditioning and environment that is ours today and that is gradually neutering us as living, sexual beings. The importance given to the problem of new reproductive techniques seems to me just one way of forcing women back into their role as mothers and defining the couple as merely a reproductive unit. There are many more urgent tasks awaiting us on our planet if we are to resist technical imperialism. Women have been merely tools in the feeding and tending of the family and society. Animals fulfill these functions as well as humans, and sometimes in the animal kingdom the tasks are divided up more fairly and the courtship displays are more aesthetic. By contrast, the identity of the human female is unknown or has become unknown. The society, the culture function according to male paradigms: genealogical paradigms and sexual paradigms.

Let me give some examples from different areas, both theoretical and practical. Each example will be matched with a suggestion for cultural change.

1. The first examples are related to the mythological, religious, and symbolic foundations of our social and cultural order.

• In all public places, whether civil or religious, it is always a question of the man's father or mother.

• In the societies that are labeled matrilinear, power in fact belongs to the *male* genealogy in the mother's family: it is the mother's brother who is responsible and valued in the society and therefore the *son*, not the daughter, and this intervention of the son breaks the cultural thread between mother and daughter.

• The incest taboo between mother and son or between sister and brother is the basis of all social order, according to anthropology.

• The relationships of father to son and mother to son are the dominant models for our religions. Obviously, the father-son relationship is considered more perfect but, for Christianity, the mother-son couple represents the couple of the incarnation of God, and it figures in almost all places of worship and is quoted in all Christian services.

• According to Freud, the mother-son relationship is the most perfect paradigm of desire, and the love between a woman and a man is possible only when the woman has become the mother of a son and can therefore carry over to her husband the feelings she experiences for her male child.

• Etc.

This is all part of the same sociocultural patterns. But very few students of myth have laid bare the origins, the qualities and functions, the events that led up to the disappearance of the great mother-daughter couples of mythology: Demeter-Kore, Clytemnestra-Iphigenia, Jocasta-Antigone, to mention only a few famous Greek figures that have managed to leave some traces in patriarchal times.

I suggest that those of you who care about social justice should put up posters in public places showing beautiful images of that natural and spiritual couple, the mother-daughter, the couple that testifies to a very special relationship to nature and culture. Our churches, our town halls are bare of such images. This indicates a cultural injustice that we can easily remedy. No wars, no dead, no wounded will result. We can do this before we undertake the reform of the language, since that will take much longer. This cultural restoration will begin to heal a loss of individual and collective identity for women. It will heal many of women's ills—not just distress but competitiveness and destructive aggressiveness. It will help women move out of the private into the public sphere, out of the family into the society where they live. The mother-daughter couple is always being thrust into the background, even when some honor is paid it. Thus the event that occurred at Lourdes, which draws millions of pilgrims and tourists and is a huge money-maker, centers on the relationship of a daughter to her heavenly mother. But most of the time attention is paid to the mother without the daughter, not just in churches but on street corners, and men have taken over the cult and interfere in the relationship. Yet the event at Lourdes perhaps serves to recall the mother-daughter couple that was so important in prepatriarchal times. Who knows—perhaps it is a sign for the future. In any case, it cannot leave us indifferent.

But we must not forget that, in the time of women's law, the divine and the human were not separated by the beyond, by "heaven." This means that religion was not a realm apart that concerned something beyond the earth. The human was and was becoming divine. Moreover, the divine was always bound up with nature. The so-called supernatural meetings between mother and daughter take place in nature. Once these experiences have been fit back into institutional religious confines, however, they are not understood in the dimension of nature, although this is traditional in the religion of women. Why? On women's part, after submitting to patriarchal churches for centuries, they have become disgusted with religion and have forgotten to consider their own divine origins. The patriarchy has separated the human from the divine but it has also deprived women of their goddesses or their divinity. Before patriarchy both women and men were potentially divine, which perhaps means that they were both *social*. Every social organization is religious in most traditions. The religious is the glue that holds groups together. Under a patriarchal regime religion is expressed by rites of *sacrifice and atonement*. In the history of women religion is mixed up with the culture of the earth, the body, life, peace. Religion is the opiate of the people only because it is imposed upon us as the religion of the race of men. In fact, it is one dimension of social organization. But it is completely different in regard to the divinization, here and now, of sexed bodies. That exists in cultures in which women are not excluded from social organization. In India, for example, and at the beginnings of our Greek culture—and we are, in large part, Indo-Europeans—sexuality was cultural and sacred. It also constituted an important reservoir of energy for both men and women. The patriarchy has taken the divine away from women. It has carried it off and made it an all-men affair, and it often accuses the religious spirit of women of being the devil's work.

But few scholars or theologians have investigated the relation of mother-daughter couples to fertility and respect for nature. Those women who remain close to nature after a certain period are called witches, sorceresses, whereas, at the beginning of our history the mother-daughter couple simply represents the place where the cult of the body and of natural elements can be held. The magic, the burned offerings, the sacrificial and propitiatory rites occur only after a break has occurred in this relation to nature: the only universal capable of being immediate and mediatized at one and the same time, with no recourse to hermetic or occult practices.

The religion of men masks an act of dispossession that has broken the relation to the natural universe and perverted its simplicity. Clearly, religion is a figure for a social universe organized by men. But this organization is founded upon a sacrifice: of nature, of the sexed body, especially of women. It imposes a spirituality that has been cut off from its roots in the natural environment. Thus it cannot fulfill humanity. To spiritualize, to socialize, to cultivate, we must start off from what is. Patriarchal regimes do not do this because they seek to conceal the ways in which they have imposed their authority: 1) a usurpation of the power of the other sex and 2) by massively favoring the family over the sexed couple.

If today we put up pictures of mother-daughter couples—photos, paintings, sculptures, but not ads—in all our public places, we would be showing respect for the social order. This last is not formed of mothers and *sons*, as patriarchal culture would have us believe, with all the virginal ideals that culture reserves for itself and which it often equates with money, with its reproductive goals, its incestuous games, and its reduction of love to natural fruitfulness and the discharge of social entropy, etc.

Women's inability to organize, to understand one another and find a common will makes some people smile and deeply discourages others. But how could women unite when they lack any representation or example of that alliance? This lack has not always existed. There was once a time when mother and daughter formed a paradigm for nature and for society. This couple was the guardian of nature's fruitfulness in general and of the relation to the divine. During that era food consisted of the fruits of the earth. Thus the mother-daughter couple guaranteed human food supplies and was also the place where oracles were spoken. This couple watched over the memory of the past: then the daughter respected her mother, her genealogy. The couple also cared for the present: food was brought forth by the earth in serenity and peace. Foreseeing the future occurred thanks to women's relation to the divine, to the word of the oracle.

Were men harmed by this organization? No. When life, love, and nature are respected neither sex is destroyed by the other. The two

191

sexes loved each other without need of the institution of matrimony, without obligation to bear children—though this never meant that no children were born—without censorship of sex and body.

This is probably what monotheistic religions tell as the myth of the earthly paradise. This myth corresponds to the many centuries of history that we now label prehistory, primitive times, etc. Those people who lived in those so-called archaic times were perhaps more cultivated than we are. We retain some traces of them in art: temples, sculptures, paintings, but also myths and tragedies, particularly those that express the passage into the historical era. This can be dated for us at the beginning of the golden age of the Greeks. Certain Far Eastern traditions have kept the prepatriarchal heritage much longer.

The beginning of the patriarchal power that we are familiar with—i.e., of the male's power as legal head of the family, of the tribe, the race, the State—is associated with the dispersal of women into isolated homes, and most particularly the separation of the daughter from her mother. This relationship, which is the most fertile in regard to safeguarding life and peace, was destroyed for an order to be established that is linked to private property, to the transmission of goods from father to son, to the institution of monogamous marriage—which ensures that all property, including children, can be passed down the male line—and to the establishment of social organizations open to men alone and designed for the same purposes.

2. I shall therefore take my next examples from the area of the law. in fact, we need to be wary of accepting the *written* representativeness of the law of women. It is incredible but nonetheless true that unisexual theory and practice can be made into law and enforced. This was possible only because women have been separated from their mothers, isolated from one another, and deprived of a culture of their own. But in order to create a culture one has to have the right to assemble, to speak together, to organize freely and independently of economic, legal, and religious barriers.

All women, however, are still in such a state of social and cultural bondage, even when they believe they are free and emancipated. Why is this so? Because the order that lays down the law to us is of the male sex. The few individual advantages women have won have not changed the situation much. Many people like to boast that all the female or feminist struggles are at an end. If this were true it would mean that women have never really struggled, that they had set themselves the wrong goal. Social and cultural acceptance of sexual difference has not been achieved and this can be the only goal of a movement for women's liberation.

As far as I can see, the main real condition of liberation that women have demanded is the right to contraception and abortion, a right that many governments are ready to revoke. This right is merely testimony that women's lives are respected, that they need no longer submit to reproduction and to continuing their husbands' genealogy. This right has to be matched by legal protection afforded to women in cases of rape. The law must give equal weight to the violence, often even the crimes, the blows, the wounds women suffer in private and in public. These are elementary rights that must be inscribed in the body of law if women are to be recognized as full citizens.

The law has a sex, justice has a sex, but by default:

1) The law was written by a race of men acting almost like slave-holders in regard to sexual difference: the woman will leave her family, will live with her husband, will take his name, will allow herself to be possessed by him physically, will bear his children, and bring them up—which means nursing, cooking, washing, doing housework, all boring and repetitive jobs such as arouse contempt or pity when performed by working men. Are we to say that woman finds advantages in this system because her husband is working for her? My answer would be that this division of labor not only treats woman as a child (children also are provided for by their parents and the State while they work in what amounts to an educational apprenticeship) but also corrupts her mind far more deeply than is the case with workers who are employed in capitalist industry and commerce. The fact of being paid by their husbands makes women forget the respect and rights due to their sex, to their mothers, to all women, and even makes them, today, careless of life itself. To any-one capable of looking at this human dimension with some measure of objectivity, the difference between the sexes has been reduced to a matter of money, just like everything else.

2) The second major characteristic of patriarchal law, in fact, is that it is almost entirely concerned with questions of property. In

law the individual is defined in terms of his relation to possession. He must submit to this. The race of men are blind to the meaning of their patriarchal foundations, and thus unaware that, originally, the privilege of capital concerns man alone. Politicians and scholars argue learnedly about the fact that wealth, which is supposedly genderless, must be divided equally. But wealth must be understood to mean the accumulation of goods through exploitation, and to be the outcome of one sex's submission to the other. Capitalization is, indeed, what organizes patriarchal power as such, through the mechanization of our sexed bodies and the injustice caused by the dominance over those bodies.

The race of men have always put property before life. Men care little about living matter and its cultural economy. The society of men is built upon the possession of goods. Life itself is equated with property, with productive capital, possessed as a work tool not as the basis of the identity to be cultivated. The patriarchy has no interest in spiritualizing sexed nature. Therefore patriarchy's relation to matter and its cultural organization is twisted. Hegel in particular was aware of this ethical failure in our relations to the natural world and to genders and their genealogies: Antigone is sacrificed because she respects the blood and the gods of her mother and therefore performs the rites over her dead brother. Hegel has written that the whole subsequent development of the spirit was mortgaged against this original sacrifice. As for Marx, he pays great attention to the social economy but very little to the culture of nature, except insofar as nature has been transformed into utilities and thus lost as a natural phenomenon. Thus we have been encouraged to discuss social justice at length without recalling that social justice has its roots in and takes its strength from nature. This is particularly obvious for women in their reproductive capacity, for primary materials and arable land, but it is also true for all bodies. There can be no society without bodies to compose it. This tautology is always being forgotten under pressure from the subjective male economy, at least in our patriarchal cultures.

3. My third example will therefore concern the issue of the difference between men and women in subject-object and subject-subject relations. The society of men presents certain traits that are sup-

posed to be universal but are the outcome of the sex of those who make up the society.

Thus, for lack of a sexual culture and of a method for achieving cultural relations between the genders (a partially dialectic method), man—in his logic, his speech, his behavior, his whole subjective economy—wavers endlessly between the *yes* and the *no* that he says to the part played by the mother, in all her various definitions, in constituting his identity. These contradictory oscillations become more and more anarchic as they develop. The rhythm of yes and no moves out of the control of the speaker. Man needs these switches between yes and no so that he can maintain a distance from the matter that created him. Most often, he tries to retain his attitude of denial toward the primary mother or matrix. By different means that include highly sophisticated argument, man refuses reality and tries to impose a *second nature* that ends up destroying and burying the first. This process corresponds to the culture or the history of a given era. Then nature reclaims her rights. But for this process to continue, some natural reserves must always be available; that may no longer be the case today. What we call human nature often implies forgetting or misunderstanding our being as bodies in the name of some deceptive or perverse spirituality. Actually, who knows what human nature is? Presumably some kind of hypothesis needed for patriarchy to function, since this same human nature takes no account of sexual difference in its definition of cultural identity. The duty to bear children and stay in the home does not amount to a female identity. At best a function or a social role.

Woman is far from being in the same type of subjective identity as man. In actual fact, in order to have access to her own sexuality, she does not have to put a distance between herself and her mother through a *yes* or a *no*, a *near* or a *far*, an *inside* or an *outside*. She has to be or become a woman like her mother, and, at the same time, be able to differentiate and distance herself from her mother. But her mother is like herself. She cannot be reduced or manipulated like an *object* as she is by the little boy or the man. According to Freud, and more generally according to other theories of sexuality, our desire is the desire for objects and a competition for objects. Violence can be explained in terms of this need to possess objects and the competition for their possession. The status and even the identity of an individual is defined by the objects belonging to him. This economy has some validity for male subjectivity. The woman, however, becomes a subject immediately through her relation to a subject like herself: her mother. She cannot reduce her mother to the status of an object without reducing herself at the same time, because she and her mother share the same sex. Hence it is the law that female desire be for all or nothing if it fails to find a subjective identity through the relationship to the mother. The *fort-da*, which Freud describes as marking the child's entry into the world of language and culture, does not work for the girl child, unless she identifies herself as a little boy. Then she loses herself in a male other, and makes her children, and subsequently her husband, into quasi objects. In this way she appears to act in accordance with the phallic patterns that have been ascribed to her. But this has nothing to do with her identity.

Confusing *identity* and *identification* does not amount to finding an order for the matter and its form that we are. It is an idealist trap that leads to much social entropy. The neuter often comes in here: in the confusion of identity and identification. The deceptive notion of obscurely being or potentially being men, and vice versa, condemns many women to self-exile and turns them into agents of social and individual destruction. All the same, women are not attuned to or in agreement with the forces of destruction. The possible discovery of women's identity, on the other hand, raises an important problem of subjective relationship. It would seem that woman enters directly into intersubjective rapport with her mother. Her economy is based on *subject-subject* relations, not subject-object, and is thus a highly social and cultural economy that leads to women being interpreted as the guardians of love. This subjective economy between mother and daughter can be partially translated into nonverbal communication, and has thus been subject to criticism from women and men who misunderstand or deny for various reasons the need for a sexually differentiated discourse. Woman needs to develop words, images, and symbols to express her intersubjective relationship with her mother, and then with other women, if she is to enter into a nondestructive relation with men. We need to release, examine, and define this economy of identity that is specific to woman. This is indispensable if we are to have a livable culture. This in turn depends upon us supporting, not destroying, the mother-daughter relationship. We must cease to assume that the daughter must turn away from her mother to obey her father or to love her husband. If a sexual identity is to be built, a genealogical relationship with one's own gender and a respect for both genders are essential. This in turn demands that we establish viable erotic paradigms rather than neu-tralizing, unrepressing, or desublimating the sexes in the ways we have become accustomed to.

4. What sexual patterns prevail at the moment? Male sexuality—and according to Freud there is no other kind—is built upon a dynamic model in which energy builds up and is released, returning the organism to homeostasis. This economy is based upon the two principles of thermodynamics that have long been considered insur-mountable. So, according to this theory, sexuality is linked to the laws of physics and thus has no freedom and a future that involves only repetition and explosion, never evolution. The only way to escape this sad fate would be procreation. It is true that Freud gives no hints as to how sublimation proceeds in adult life. Becoming man or woman would merely mean becoming reproductive units, with no energy to spare for thinking, sharing, growing with the other sex. According to this specialist in sexuality, only the partial drives have the capacity to be sublimated. Perhaps this notion explains why Freud is so regressive in both his theory and his practice even as he proclaims his dissatisfaction with a simple genital reproductive model for human sexuality.

What do we mean by partial drives? Freud is particularly inter-ested in *sight*, but hearing, smell, and touch are also partial drives. Touch, which has a part to play in all the senses, constitutes a very special sense and Freud has little to say about it. He is too concerned with objects. Touch is a more subjective, intersubjective sense; it lies between the active and the passive; it eludes the economy of war, possessions, and mechanics, except when it is reduced to blows and wounds or to a part of the body.

But does this possible sublimation of the senses stand today? The energy of tension, discharge, return to homeostasis is competitive with technology, but the return to equilibrium and stability is be-coming increasingly problematic and thus technology is advancing faster and stronger everyday. We have to get on the ball, keep things hopping, keep with the beat or whatever—otherwise everything goes to hell in a handbasket. These drives demand a stronger and stronger discharge and compete among themselves. But this race toward human and technical entropy makes us forget that we are living beings. We are sacrificing ourselves on the altar of this *pathos*, this

unregulated drive for more and more energy, more and more economic, individual, and collective growth. We are out of tune with
our natural rhythms.

All this emotion, this private and public feeling (often roused in
us as unwary and passive consumers by a publicity machine devoted
to the interests of industry and commerce) seems to move into the
vacant place left by the forgotten body. That body relates much
more to *perception* than to *pathos*. A body breathes, feels, tastes, sees,
hears, touches, is touched. These bodily attributes have almost disappeared. But how do we live without our bodies? What can this
extinction mean? It means that male culture has so polluted our air,
our food, our sight, our hearing, our touch, that our senses are close
to destruction. Yet we can neither live nor think without the mediation of our senses.

As far as sound is concerned, doctors are well aware that we are
in the process of losing our hearing, and their clinical observations
merely confirm what each of us knows from experience and good
sense. Our ears are constantly bombarded with machine noise, even
from the sky above, and they lose their acuity as a kind of self-
defense. The ears also suffer from the extreme speeds and the fre-
quent changes in altitude that we subject them to in air travel and
other contemporary modes of transport. Now, our ears are our most
important organs for balance and for thermal and affective regulation. This means that we cannot ask a group of people to be peaceful
and cooperative, much less affectionate, if they are being constantly
shocked and upset by an acoustic barrage. This is particularly true
for women whose hearing is more sensitive than men's, and who are
being assaulted by noise even in their homes, given the growing
number of technical devices and the increasing noise from roads and
airlanes. Noise attacks and other forms of sense pollution are no
longer limited to a few groups of workers. They affect the whole
population, and there is no compensation in the form of salary or
anything else. When we destroy our acoustic perceptions, we destroy
a good part of our identity. Furthermore, hearing is the sense that
we develop passively and at the earliest stage in our development
(the foetus can hear in the mother's womb) but it is also the sense
that occupies the highest and most universal levels of culture—
verbal communication and listening to music. Thus it is imperative
that we find an economy of noise that protects our hearing. Several
quite simple and even inexpensive means exist: limit the number of

roads open to vehicular traffic, both inside and outsde towns, establish pedestrian precincts and silence zones, cease to exploit the whole sky for air lanes, direct research toward the development of silent machines. Some machines of this kind already exist, and these are vital priorities that must be respected, even at the loss of a little acceleration or at the cost of teaching consumers to go a few yards on foot—life-saving measures, in and of themselves.

As for sight, our eyes are losing their elasticity because they are dazzled by the public lighting that is more and more common and harsh. The materials used today for the windows in large buildings and particularly in cars make solar reverberations more and more difficult to bear. Even as the sales of sun glasses and other devices soar, our bodies and our sensitivies are nonetheless being ravaged.

I shall not go on with this dismal litany. You all know as well as I do that food is getting more tasteless and even toxic because of the chemical additives, the growth hormones administered to animals, and the treatment they are subjected to. We have to walk a long way before we smell something good, and smell is crucial to our vitality and the very air, the most vital matter, is so polluted by toxins of every kind that it risks losing its essential qualities. Here again, just as it is fair to denounce the deadly use of air in time of war so I feel we need to spend more energy demanding the right to breathe clean air in peacetime. Even as we maintain our vigilance toward certain potential dangers, we must not neglect the permanent bodily destruction that we are undergoing in our daily lives. Particularly since there is no possible choice left, or very little. . . . Places of rest and relaxation, houses outside the city, are now also under attack from machines, cars, planes, four-wheel-drive vehicles that zip up the mountain side, dirt bikes that run races through country roads, over hills, along beaches, down river beds, etc. All such vehicles, of greater or less utility, can operate when and where they please, with very little regulation. And social hypocrisy is particularly egregious here, where, for example, young people are condemned for their crazy behavior and poor upbringing while society continues to press them with machines that upset adults and threaten lives. Our society is so concerned with making money that, in my view, only women who are conscious of the danger and anxious to preserve life are in a position to demand a restriction of technical inflation so that our bodily and mental health can be safeguarded. Even then, women have to be vigilant, they must speak out, state their desires, and they must be able to express themselves in public and get a hearing.

Women do not obey the same sexual economy as men. I have written a great deal on this subject. To summarize in just a few words, women have different relations to fluids and solids, to matter and to form, to touch, to symmetry, to repetition, etc. In the context of this talk I mainly want to remind you that women do not have the same relation to entropy, homeostasis, and discharge. They have a much stronger internal regime, which keeps them in a constant and irreversible pattern of growth. This is not necessarily negative: it is not necessarily a matter of degeneration or accumulation. A woman enters puberty, is deflowered, becomes pregnant once or many times, goes through menopause, etc., and all these events mark a much more continuous temporality than does the pattern of masculine sexuality, which is either ruptured or else continues with no irreversible event. This female temporality is hormonally complex and in turn has consequences for the organization and general equilibrium of the body. But every stage in this development has its own temporality, which is possibly cyclic and linked to cosmic rhythms. If women have felt so terribly threatened by the accident at Chernobyl, that is because of the irreducible relation of their bodies to the universe. In fact, this component in their sexed development has trouble adapting to the acceleration in which technology involves us. A pregnancy always requires the same amount of time, as does the menstrual cycle. Thus women are constrained to obey a *double temporality*. In certain places it has become a moving anachronism even to see a pregnant women. All the same, society demands that women become pregnant, and the medical assistance women receive does not cover the affective, nervous, and hormonal problems they face. Furthermore, the intervention of the medical profession, although obviously necessary in certain cases, causes women to feel a loss of responsibility and identity when the pace of life and its harmful results makes medical care indispensable and permanent.

I know that this relation to natural temporality has meant that women have sometimes been considered a brake on culture, as "reactionaries," and that women see themselves in this way. I am not personally in agreement with this interpretation. Chernobyl and many other phenomena, some of which I have described, prove it. We need some regulation that matches the rhythms of nature: we need to cultivate this affiliation with nature and not to destroy it in order to impose a double nature that has been split off from our bodies and their elementary environment. Woman suffer more grievously from the rupture with cosmic checks and balances. Therefore it is up to women to say *no*. Without a *yes* from women the world of men cannot continue and develop. Obviously, we need to learn when and why to say this *no*. We also need to know how to say it. All this requires an apprenticeship in the subjectivity-objectivity relation that women particularly lack because in the past they have been identified as the object of desire. This apprenticeship is a practical possibility. It has to become part of the curriculum in the political and cultural education of girls. I shall immediately offer you one small example of a possible way to distance oneself, from an authority figure who lays down the law to us, and from oneself as listening and speaking subject.

☆

5. My example will focus on the interesting way we can use very simple linguistic and logical theories to learn how to analyze a speech act, how not listen to it in a credulous or passive manner, and how to identify the sex of the speaker and his or her relation to the other sex and to the world.

Of course, we ought to recognize up front that language is not neutral, and that its rules weigh heavily upon the constitution of a female identity and of the relations of women amongst themselves.

What does it mean to say that language is not neutral? Some very simple things at first: a) in many languages, such as French and Italian, a mixed group of men and women is always referred to in the masculine form: "Electeurs et electrices, vous etes tous des *Italiens*"—if Italian women want to remain grammatically feminine, they have to be female down to the last woman; (b) in patriarchal cultures realities that are valued usually are given the masculine gender: *le Dieu, le soleil*, etc.; (c) the neuter gender, which often appears in place of some erased sexual difference, in many languages shares the same grammatical forms as the masculine; this is true for natural phenomena (*il tonne, il vente, il fait soleil*, etc.), and for realities concerning duty or law (*il faut, il est nécessaire*, etc.). These forms of language and discourse, which seem so universal, true, and untouchable to us, are in fact determinate historical phenomena that can be changed. They obviously have an influence upon the content of discourse that differs between the sexes. I have carried out the analysis of a certain number of speech utterances by men and women and I have begun to interpret these differences, though it would take too long for me to convey my results to you today. But, since we are meeting after Chernobyl with the intention of giving serious thought to that accident, let me say that, among other things, I have analyzed certain speeches made by men in international political forums concerning nuclear arms. This scientific work, which goes beyond the normal processing by an average naive listener, proves that such political polemic is usually devoid of all content. It is true that the emptier a speech is the more we tend to project something into it. Nothingness makes us anxious, afraid, it alienates us. But I am convinced that the men who are making these speeches are quite unconscious of the meaninglessness of what they say, unaware of their own lack of subjective liberty and responsibility. They are as much at sea as we are, or even more, though they will not admit it to us or themselves. I propose that we try and escape this fascination with the vacuum, not in a spirit of aggression or revenge, but by means of rigorous analyses of speeches that lay down or comment upon social and political laws. These analyses will show that much political discourse is organized around abstract realities and an inertia of linguistic rules, with the particularity that abstract *inanimate* notions are substituted for *animate* subjects. This lends the language a magic economy. In fact, "progress." "social justice," "peace," "conflict," "armaments," etc., are not people actively responsible for the development of the society or of history but are rather so-called neutral concepts or notions into which men (and sometimes women) discharge their subjectivity, their relation to their audience, their responsibilty toward the world, out of a feeling of abstract duty that is poorly oriented in space and time. If the objection is raised that this corresponds to the style of political discourse, my reply will be that it has not always been this way but that today's leaders seem caught in the language and the culture they have produced as if in a net or in quicksand and they cannot escape. We are faced with men who are prisoners of their own civilization.

But even as certain men (and women) have chosen violence as their means of expression, often out of despair, the speeches that have no meaning in their own way constitute an appeal to violence, to war, as limits to the non-sense, to the nothingness. Talking without saying anything, especially in a situation of political mandate, entails the risk that exchanges between countries, between persons, will find forms of expression other than words. This also opens up the possibility that a dictatorial "I" will coopt the energy that has no responsible outlets and enact and enforce his own will.

When the natural spirit, the spirit particularly of the female gender, when the family spirit as understood in a certain way, are sacrificed to the neutrality of citizens devoted to service of the States, the sciences, or technology, then the social blindness of an all male society has taken the place of our life roots. This is the blindness of the libido, of argumentation, of ideas and perspectives that have been cut off from their concrete content. This blindness assumes and accelerates ignorance, misunderstanding, the destruction of the sensible world, whereas our real aim should be to find an objective and subjective articulation between nature and culture.

What advice would I give to women who seek a discourse that is neither reductive nor seductive?

a) Never give up subjective experience as an element of knowledge. The most transcendental theory is still rooted in the subjective. Truth is always the product of some man or woman. This does not mean that truth contains no objectivity.

b) Never indulge publicly in impulsive, emotive behavior; naive expressions of feeling, aggressivity, etc. Such behavior reflects the other side of the belief in an independent truth of the subject; it shows women being blindly influenced by the existing culture.

c) Work tirelessly to establish a subject-object dialectic. Apart from our own relation to the natural world, patriarchal civilization has put us in the position of objects; we need to learn to become subjects capable of speech.

d) Never accept or subscribe to the existence of a neutral, universal science, to which women should painfully gain access and with which they then torture themselves and taunt other women, transforming science into a new superego. The innocence of scientific truth is mystified quite as much as the innocence of feelings. All truth is partially relative. A theoretical truth that forces us to give up all subjective points of reference is a dangerous one.

☆

6. This leads me to my last point, which I shall merely sketch out today, since I have chosen to focus on practical ways to effect cultural change and greater justice and am therefore limiting myself to

specific sciences and fields of knowledge. The issue that will serve as my conclusion is whether the whole field of science and knowledge as we know is set up in a neutral and universal way. My answer is *no*. How could that be possible? Every piece of knowledge is produced by subjects in a given historical context. Even if that knowledge aims to be objective, even if its techniques are designed to ensure objectivity, science always displays certain choices, certain exclusions, and these are particularly determined by the sex of the scholars involved. Some contemporary epistemologists are casting doubt upon the impact of the subject, upon the object of scientific inquiry, and, in particular, research. Their questionning almost always stops short of the sexual influence of the subject. This barrier between sex and theory is very ancient. It corresponds to resistances set up in relation to established power structures and to a restricted and repressive conception of sexuality.

Now that I have sketched out the results of some of my analyses of various sectors of the human and social sciences, I think you will understand that the following data are highly pertinent to the sex of the scientific subject and to his history.

1) This subject today is enormously interested in acceleration that goes beyond our human powers, in weightlesness, in crossing through natural space and time, in overcoming cosmic rhythms and their regulation. He is also interested in disintegration, fission, explosion, catastrophes, etc. This reality can be confirmed from within the natural and the human sciences

—If the identity of the human subject is defined in the work of Freud by a *Spaltung*, this is also the word used for nuclear fission. Nietzsche also perceived his ego as an atomic nucleus threatened with explosion. As for Einstein, the main issue he raises, in my mind, is that, given his interest in accelerations without electromagnetic reequilibrations, he leaves us with only one hope, his God. It is true that Einstein played the violin: music helped him preserve his personal equilibrium. But what does the mighty theory of general relativity do for us except establish nuclear power plants and question our bodily inertia, that necessary condition of life?

—As for the astronomers, Reaves, following up on the American big bang theory, describes the origin of the universe as an explosion. How is it that this current interpretation so closely parallels the abstracts of the whole field of other scientific discoveries?

—René Thom, another theoretician who works at the intersection of science and philosophy, talks about catastrophes through conflicts rather than about generation through abundance, growth, positive attraction, particularly in nature.

—Quantum mechanics is interested in the disappearance of the world.

—Scientists today are working on smaller and smaller particles, which cannot be perceived but only defined thanks to sophisticated technical instruments and bundles of energy.

—Freud, and following him, Marcuse, are extremely pessimistic about the chances of the life drives. Yet the death drives are an individual or a collective instrument of disintegration, decomposition.

—Philosophy is very interested in the deconstruction of ontology, in the anti-, the post-, but it gives little thought to the constitution of a new, rationally founded identity.

—Sociologists cut us up into identity fragments, the semiologists into semes, relevant traits, functions, etc.

—As for psychoanalysts, and others of their kind, they refuse to acknowledge that discourse is sexualized. Yet how is sexuality to be expressed except by language? What are these wise practitioners subjecting us to as they state one truth here and disavow it over there?

—From the neurologists we get: the brain is sexualized but language is not, and in any case, it is not our problem.

So where are we to find our subjective status in all these disintegrations, these explosions, these splits or multiplicities, these losses of bodily identity? Obviously, men are doing battle here with the absolute they have created. After a propaedeutics that rigorously suppresses Truth, after the duty to remember the past, the respect for the father and for God as father, after the passage from the quantitative to the qualitative, they suggest to us as methods: "chance', "accident," "multiplicity," "pluralism," "ruptures" with the past, "forgetting," "leaps," "murders of the father," etc. Science and knowledge today constitute a real apprenticeship in the negative, with no positive horizon, a sort of ontotheology without God, at least for most scholars. But how do they articulate their knowledge, their God, with a human ethics?

Are we not faced here with an explosion or discharge of theoretical models that are too saturated or too entropic and that therefore pose a considerable threat to human bodies and human minds?

205

2) This kind of cultural semi-unrepressing often goes hand in hand with practical and theoretical contradictions, with a greater and greater distancing from our bodily matter and its qualities, with a quest for the self into abstraction and dream, with an unconsidered break with the technical environment, its influence upon us, and the ideological entropies that, in my view, can be weighed only in the culture of our *sexed* bodies.

3) Most scholars have lost control over their own discoveries, either because they have ceased themselves to perceive what they are doing and serve merely as conduits for the development of theories or techniques they have not produced, or because they are so out of touch with philosophy, with commonsense wisdom, that they are no longer thinking at all. With their microscopes or macroscopes in hand, researchers forget their bodies, forget life. This was already true for Plato. But it is a far greater threat to us now. And we have no cause for laughter.... The epistemology of the sciences is far from matching the level of technical expansion and its effects.

☆

I shall stop here for today. Perhaps you were expecting me to develop this last point further. Here with you and after Chernobyl I wanted to talk about the human realities, which require rapid changes that you can take part in. It did not seem to be ethical to go into a more sophisticated epistemological exposé without proposing some simple and effective cultural modifications that might offer you a chance for life. This is the theme of your festival and I am wholly in agreement with it.

Living entails knowing when to stop, think, and even contemplate, so that we can find our place as individuals and as a community. This is the necessary condition for a fair decision on social and cultural measures. We are in need of such contemplation today if we are to check the worldwide race into economic and cultural entropy. These are measures that women must demand, must enforce, out of respect for their bodies and their subjective liberties.